Along the **Wealdway**

We are grateful to the following bodies
for their assistance in route development
and in preparation of this guide book:

- Conservators of Ashdown Forest
- Eastbourne Borough Council
- Gravesham Highways Management Unit
- Libraries in East Sussex, Kent and West Sussex
- Kent and Sussex Areas of the Ramblers' Association and affiliated groups
- Kent Wildlife Trust
- Sussex Archaeological Society
- Sussex Downs Conservation Board
- Sussex Wildlife Trust

The development, interpretation and promotion of the Wealdway in East Sussex and Kent has been achieved with a significant financial contribution and considerable voluntary labour from Sussex and Kent Areas of the Ramblers' Association.

Supported financially by The Countryside Agency

Other Kent County Council guidebooks in this series, also available:

Eden Valley Walk
Elham Valley Way
Darent Valley Path
Greensand Way (published jointly with
Surrey County Council)
High Weald Walk
Medway Valley Walk
Stour Valley Walk

Copies of these guidebooks can be obtained from bookshops, tourist information centres, libraries and the Support Services Officer, Environmental Management Unit, Strategic Planning Directorate, Kent County Council, Invicta House, County Hall, Maidstone, Kent ME14 1XX, ☎ (01622) 221526, e-mail env.publications@kent.gov.uk

East Sussex County Council produces and publishes a series of local guides available from Countryside Management Service, East Sussex County Council, County Hall, St Anne's Crescent, Lewes, East Sussex BN7 1UE, ☎ (01273) 481654.

If you enjoy reading this guidebook and walking the Wealdway, you may be interested in seeing a video of the Walk. It is a personal view and experience of the walk from Gravesend to Eastbourne, rather than a video of the guidebook. As such it would make an ideal souvenir of your own walk. The video is available by post at £12.50 (plus £1.00 p&p) from Promo-video, PO Box 138, East Grinstead, RH19 4ZD, UK

A countryside journey across the Downs and Weald of East Sussex and Kent

Along *and* Around *the* Wealdway

Eastbourne ♦ Uckfield ♦ Tonbridge ♦ Gravesend

Produced by Rights of Way and Countryside Management Service, East Sussex County Council and Environmental Management Unit, Kent County Council.

Designed by County Print & Design, Kent County Council

Author Helen Livingston *narrative text and features*

Illustrator Matthew Cook *paintings*

Photographer Geoffrey King *photography, pen drawings and additional text*

Cartographers Ordnance Survey *route maps*

Tony Ashton and County Print & Design *additional maps*

Route maps produced by Ordnance Survey following a style developed by County Print and Design, Kent County Council. Reproduced from the Ordnance Survey Explorer maps with the permission of the Controller of Her Majesty's Stationery Office © Crown Copyright. Unauthorised reproduction infringes Crown copyright and may lead to prosecution or civil proceedings. Kent County Council licence number: LA 076708/98/06.

Ordnance Survey and Explorer are registered trademarks and the OS symbol a trademark of Ordnance Survey, the National Mapping Agency of Great Britain.

Printed in Great Britain by County Print and Design, Kent County Council.

Published jointly by Transport and Environment Department, East Sussex County Council, County Hall, St Anne's Crescent, Lewes, East Sussex BN7 1UE and Strategic Planning Directorate, Kent County Council, Invicta House, County Hall, Maidstone, Kent ME14 1XX in association with Ordnance Survey.

First published July 1999.

ISBN 0 86147 466 X *East Sussex County Council*
          1 873010 93 1 *Kent County Council*

65931/elw

Travel Guide
Contents

Wealdway
Introduction

Wealdway
A story of its people and places

To the best of our knowledge the interpretive content and all other information is believed to be correct at the time of publication. We should be grateful if you would inform us of any changes, omissions or errors, so that modifications can be made in subsequent revisions of the book.

Wealdway
Walk planning & preparation

Wealdway
Exploring the area

Further information and references

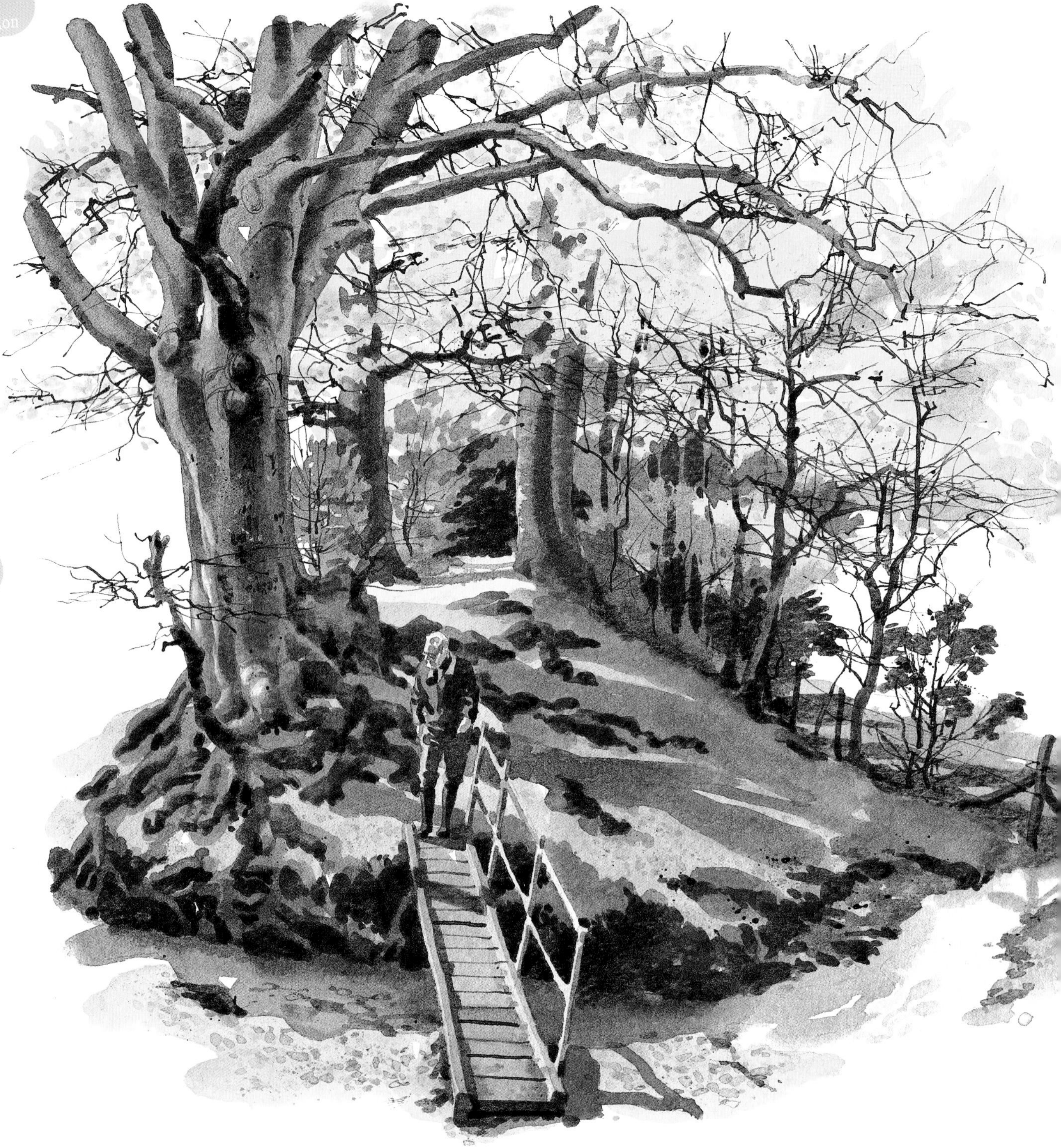

Introduction

> *The king was making for the shore*
> *But here he paused and turned his head*
> *And looked across the Weald and said*
> *'It is a land worth fighting for!'*
> Charles Duncan, on the flight of Charles II

Evocation

THE WEALDWAY runs south to north from the English Channel coast to the Thames estuary across the area of south-east England known as the Weald. It crosses the two chalk escarpments that bound the Weald to the south and north, the South and North Downs, runs through the intricate farming country of the Low Weald with its pasture-land and its patchwork of fields divided by a myriad of hedgerows and rises up over the sandstone rocks of the High Weald at Ashdown Forest, where there are wide views across the region.

The name 'Weald' comes from the Anglo-Saxon 'Andreds-Weald', the name they gave to the great forest that in those days clothed the region. Even today the Weald is surprisingly well-wooded, giving from viewpoints such as the downs and Ashdown Forest, an undeniable

Avery's Wood, Bullingstone

sensation that the spirit of Andredsweald is alive and well. These woodlands include shaws and coppices, hedgerows and scraps of ancient woodland whose boundaries have not changed in a thousand years. It is a region of farmsteads, hamlets and villages. Apart from Eastbourne and Gravesend at the two ends of the walk, Tonbridge is the only large town on the Wealdway. Uckfield, Hailsham and Royal Tunbridge Wells are close by.

Eastbourne is a fitting beginning or end to the Wealdway, for it fronts the sea and looks south towards continental Europe. The sea and Europe have played a large part in the history of the Weald, beginning in Roman times when the Weald's iron and timber went to help maintain the Roman fleet. Gravesend, at the northern end of the walk, lies on the Thames estuary and looks one way towards London and the other to the world.

View from the South Downs near Folkington

7

8

Geology

THE WEALD is one of the most fascinating geological regions in Europe. Once a great dome of land, capped by chalk rocks, it has now been stripped bare so that the chalk – the North and South Downs – forms a rim. The land between these chalk escarpments is the Weald.

The geological structure of the Weald is relatively simple in overall design but complicated in detail. The basic structure is that of a denuded dome which produces east-west directional ridges. The oldest rocks, mostly sandstones, are exposed in the centre, in a swathe of country stretching from Horsham in the west to Hastings in the east, including the wild tracts of Ashdown Forest. This is the High Weald, sometimes known as the 'Forest Ridges'. The High Weald is heavily folded and faulted. It is flanked by extensive vales of Weald Clay, to the south the Vale of Sussex, to the north the Vale of Kent.

Deep weathering of the sandstone along vertical joints has resulted in strangely-shaped masses jutting out from hillsides, such as the Toad Rock on Rusthall Common near Royal Tunbridge Wells, as well as sandstone cliffs as at High Rocks and Harrisons Rocks.

Wealden rivers, inherited from the days of the Wealden dome, tend to flow either north or south, depending on which side of the High Weald watershed they rise. Thus, the River Medway flows north cutting through the North Downs to reach the Thames estuary, while the Cuckmere River flows south and cuts through the South Downs to the English Channel.

Geological map of the Downs and Weald

Clay, Sand & Gravel | Chalk | Gault Clay | Lower Greensand | Weald Clay & Sand

Geological cross section across the Downs and Weald

| THAMES BASIN River Thames | NORTH DOWNS | GREENSAND RIDGE | CENTRAL WEALD | SOUTH DOWNS |

Overlying rocks removed by erosion following folding and uplift

Older underlying rocks

North	KENT/SURREY			EAST SUSSEX	South
Clay, Sand & Gravel	Chalk	Gault Clay		Lower Greensand	Weald Clay & Sand

Areas of outstanding *natural beauty*

THE WEALDWAY passes through four areas that enjoy protected status, the Sussex Heritage Coast and three Areas of Outstanding Natural Beauty (AONBs), the Sussex Downs, the High Weald and the Kent Downs.

The Sussex Heritage Coast runs for 8 miles (13km) along one of the world's most famous shorelines. It includes the spectacular chalk cliffs of Beachy Head and the Seven Sisters, and is one of the last stretches of undeveloped coastline in south-east England. The Heritage Coast zone extends sea-wards as a marine conservation area, as well as inland to include delicate downland habitats.

The Sussex Downs AONB covers 384 square miles (983sq km) and runs along the South Downs westwards from Beachy Head, where the downs plunge into the sea, to the Hartings, on the border with Hampshire. The Sussex Downs Conservation Board aims to manage and maintain surviving patches of the short sweet downland turf with its numerous wildflowers and rare butterflies.

The High Weald AONB covers 570 square miles (1,460sq km) of the Weald's sandstone core, a region of rolling hills, steep ridges and deep thickly wooded ghylls. The AONB is characterised by an intricate landscape of small fields fringed by hedgerows with small villages of white weatherboarded cottages and traditional oast houses. It also includes the ecologically important ancient woodland and heaths of Ashdown Forest.

The Kent Downs AONB

Ashdown Forest

runs along the Kent section of the North Downs and covers 343 square miles (878sq km). On the crest of the downs are stretches of open downland turf where orchids bloom, while the steep southward facing chalk scarps are famed for their ancient bluebell woods. The Wealdway crosses a characteristic section of this AONB, climbing the scarp through bluebell woods and passing through attractive historic villages and close to great houses with their attendant parks.

Map of the Areas of Outstanding Natural Beauty

TILBURY
GREATER LONDON
GRAVESEND
DARTFORD
Swanley
Longfield
ROCHESTER
GILLINGHAM
CHATHAM
Biggin Hill
SEVENOAKS
Leybourne
Oxted
Borough Green
Limpsfield
Godstone
TONBRIDGE
MAIDSTONE
Lingfield
Edenbridge
Paddock Wood
Headcorn
EAST GRINSTEAD
ROYAL TUNBRIDGE WELLS
Tenterden
Cranbrook
HAYWOODS HEATH
Wadhurst
CROWBOROUGH
High Weald
BURGESS HILL
UCKFIELD
Heathfield
Battle
LEWES
HASTINGS
BRIGHTON
HAILSHAM
BEXHILL
Peacehaven
NEWHAVEN
Sussex Downs
SEAFORD
EASTBOURNE
Sussex Heritage Coast
Kent Downs
Wealdway

Natural history

THE VARIED LANDSCAPE of the Weald ensures a variety of different habitats: coastal, estuarine, freshwater, chalkland, heathland, clay lowland, farmland and urban. The natural vegetation is deciduous woodland; the High Weald or Forest Ridges once supported great forests, from St Leonards in the west to Ashdown Forest and beyond. In AD731 the Venerable Bede described the Wealden Forest as "thick and impenetrable". This was dense secondary woodland much of which had overrun erstwhile farmland since the collapse of Roman rule in Britain in AD410. The timber was removed for building and for fuel for the once-flourishing iron industry, as well as for ships, although Baltic oak was much preferred by the Navy. From the 18th century onwards trees have been planted and today the Weald has a more wooded appearance than at any time since the Middle Ages. In the clay vales, oaks – frequently referred to as 'Sussex Weed' – are the dominant tree. Until recently most of the woodlands were coppiced, leading to a distinctive mix of wildlife, including badgers, squirrels and deer.

The open heathlands of Ashdown Forest, the second largest heath in southern England, support a particularly notable birdlife with nesting species including stonechats, nightjars, tree pipits and hobbys. The coarse sands of the Lower Greensand are noted for their heathlands, particularly in Kent, though these habitats are declining with increased forestry. The heavy waterlogged soils of the Weald Clay traditionally support deciduous woodlands and small pastures separated by hedgerows supporting a rich wildlife, though today many bigger fields exist, many miles of hedgerow having been destroyed in the process.

On the chalklands there is now much arable farming and the short sweet turf associated with sheep rearing is reduced to mere fragments. The decline in grazing also means the increase in chalk scrubland of hawthorn, blackthorn and wild rose. Birds of the open downland include skylarks, wheatears and goldfinches. Lullington Heath on the South Downs is a rare tract of chalk heathland, where a thin capping of acidic soil enables heathland plants like heather to flourish on an alkaline bedrock. In the damp river valleys of the Cuckmere and the Medway, whitebeam and lime trees grow and frogs and toads are found.

Flock of sheep on the road, Chiddingly

Brown's Brook, near Fairwarp

Land
use

L AND USE in the Weald varies greatly with the underlying rocks, but it is true to say that woodland management and woodland crafts are still a feature of the Wealden economy. Trees have been felled here since neolithic times and during Roman times timber was an important product, along with charcoal for the numerous iron works. Coppicing, an ancient technique involving cropping every 12 to 20 years, has provided fuel and fencing for generations. The steady clearance of the Andredsweald accelerated through the Middle Ages, till by Tudor times most of the forest had vanished. From the 18th century replanting has taken place, initially of

Hop pickers, Peckham Place Farm

hardwoods and more recently conifers.

The Great Storm of 1987 devastated many fine Wealden woodlands, but improved woodland management is healing the scars and the burgeoning herb layer has flourished, particularly the vast swathes of springtime bluebells.

Agriculture in the Weald is governed by the soil, so that today the chalk downland rims are largely under cereals, the huge sheep flocks of yesteryear having been evicted by the plough. The sandy soils of the High Weald have traditionally supported mixed farms, with plenty of rough grazing as well as cereals, fruit and hops. This pattern has been squeezed by modern farming methods in the last twenty years but some traditional orchards remain. Widespread pasturelands are found in the Low Weald, where there are also traditional mixed farms.

The heavy soils of the Gault Clay,

Orchard route near Barnes Street

in particular the Vale of Homesdale, support woodland and pastureland, while the Wealdway runs through that part of Kent traditionally dubbed the 'Garden of England', the area to the west of Maidstone where, until recently, half of England's apple orchards were to be found.

The most notable Wealden industry in the past was iron, mined here since prehistoric times but especially during the Roman era and in the 17th century. The iron industry is associated in particular with the High Weald and there are many clues left in the landscape. Ordnance – cannon and

shot – were the chief products, with a lucrative sideline in firebacks, railings and other iron goods.

Extractive industries, other than the mining of iron ore, traditionally include the quarrying of building materials, of which there are many types. In the past flints were quarried from the chalk and in places chalk itself was cut for use as a building stone. Today Kentish ragstone, that famous building stone once carried down the River Medway to build London, notably the Tower of London, is still mined from the Lower Greensand while Ashdown Sand and Tunbridge Wells Sand are also quarried. Ballast is also extracted from river gravels, particularly along the River Medway, where building and silica sand are also quarried.

The Weald Clay has for generations been the source of tiles and bricks as well as other earthenware items, and there were formerly many tile and brick-works making tiles and bricks and chimney pots, as at Berwick and Uckfield. Several remain today whereas the potteries, like the famous Dicker Pottery, have sadly passed away.

11

History &
Archaeology

THE WEALDWAY passes through two counties, East Sussex and Kent, both ancient kingdoms. The kingdom of the South Saxons, Sussex, was founded in AD477. At this time the dense scrubby woodland of the Forest of Andredsweald separated the two kingdoms. Kent comes from the Cantii, the Iron Age tribe who inhabited it prior to the Roman conquest. The kingdom of Kent was established early in Saxon times and under Ethelbert (AD560-616) rose to supremacy over most of England.

The prehistory of the Weald makes a fascinating tale, with evidence of mesolithic settlements at High Rocks and at Garden Hill on Ashdown Forest. There are many neolithic sites, some along the Medway valley, while the many impressive neolithic long barrows, such as Coldrum Stones and Hunter's Burgh, are found on the chalk hills. Recently an important Bronze Age site has been excavated at Willingdon Levels near Eastbourne, the first to be found in the South East. There are numerous Iron Age (Celtic) sites, particularly on the South Downs above Eastbourne. During Roman times the High Weald was an important 'Black Country' producing iron, while corn was grown in large quantities on the chalk downlands, much as it is today. Many villas have been found, and the region was well served by major and minor roads. In Ashdown Forest, the Wealdway runs along the Roman London-Lewes Way.

The wooded nature of the Weald, and its notoriously bad roads, frequently quagmires, meant that although close to London, the Weald remained remote and rural. Thus, it is not surprising to find it associated with smuggling and other unlawful activities. Indeed two of the most notorious of all 18th-century smuggling gangs, those of Groombridge and Hawkurst, were based in the region.

During the Middle Ages the Weald again became an important industrial centre, producing iron, timber and pottery, heavy goods that were mostly transported by river and shipped round the coast. With the cutting down of the forest, and the building of the turnpike roads and later the railways, the Weald was finally tamed, and today its isolated and remote past is little more than a memory.

Coldrum Stones, Trottiscliffe, Kent

Architecture

THE DIVERSITY of Wealden rocks has led to the use of a wide range of different building materials. However, as is only to be expected in such a wooded landscape, the traditional building materials were wood, bricks and tiles. Timber-framed houses remain, many of which are traditional 15th-century 'Wealden' type hall-houses, with big curved braces, such as Filching Manor, Horselunges and Stonehill Farm. There are brick-built houses of Tudor age, like Place Farm at Chiddingly, and a whole range of cottage styles with hung-tiles. These days it is rare to see a thatched cottage in the Weald, but once it was the most common roofing. It has now been almost universally replaced by tiles or even slates.

On the chalklands flint was used as a building material, and most downland churches, as well as those in the vales near to downland, were built of flint. Stone, where available, was used for more important buildings, churches and, in particular, grand houses, including the magnificent Tonbridge Castle, built in Kentish ragstone

Withyham church

Timber-framed house, Tonbridge

13

Wealdway ~ *A story of its people and places*

The Downs and the Sea

Eastbourne to Upper Dicker

> *The hills look over on the south*
> *And southward dreams the sea...*
> Francis Thompson

THIS STRETCH OF THE WEALDWAY crosses the South Downs, the open, treeless chalk uplands which descends into the secretive country of the clay Weald. The downs were once famous for their roaming flocks of Southdown sheep but now the sheep are few and the downs present a tapestry of arable fields and short grassland, blown and rippled by the wind, tangy with the salt spray of the English Channel. The South Downs look north to the Weald and south to the sea. They have endured a long history of human occupation, indeed the very word 'down' is a rare Celtic survival in the Saxon south-east, coming from 'dun' (fort). Today these great rounded hills stand bare of habitation, the villages and hamlets tucked neatly into the valleys, coombes and hollows. Flint, timber and sometimes chalk itself are used in building, while many cottages are tile-hung in the Sussex fashion.

Please note that the numbers in blue boxes correspond to the selected features in the walk guide and the sequence of letters and numbers in brackets is the Ordnance Survey grid reference of a feature.

14

Eastbourne

church of St Mary **11**, with its massive tower. Marine Parade is on the site of Seahouses, the original watering-place, where George III's children stayed in 1780.

Today the resort is famed for its flowery promenade **2**, for its spacious hotels gazing over the Channel, for the beauty of its nearby downland and for its weather – "the sunniest of all England's seaside resorts" is the proud boast.

Eastbourne's three-tiered promenade, bedecked with colourful flower gardens and fountains, retains an aura of refinement. Here is the bandstand, opposite a seated figure of the 7th Duke of Devonshire. Further east is the Victorian pier **1**, where the Wealdway starts and finishes (the attractive iron-work and coloured glass fittingly reminding us of the ancient Wealden industries), and the imposing Redoubt Fortress (TV 623997) built, with its accompanying Martello towers, against Napoleon.

During the 20th century Eastbourne has twice had to don battle-dress, and was one of the worst bombed of coastal towns during the Second World War.

The South Downs finally plunge to the sea at Beachy Head **12**, at 536 feet (165m), the highest cliff on England's south coast. For centuries the particular dread of mariners, it is still something of a fearful spot. Beachy Head (from 'Beau Chef' – 'beautiful headland',

Eastbourne

Eastbourne was born of the sea, not of seafaring but of the 18th-century craze for sea-bathing: the name itself conjures up visions of English seaside holidays. It passed its infancy as a rather discreet watering place, patronised by Royalty and the well-to-do, grew up and came of age during the 1850s with its grand development by the local landowners, William Cavendish, later the 7th Duke of Devonshire and the Gilberts of Eastbourne Place.

There are remains of Roman villas under the streets of Eastbourne, but these were ruinous before 'Bourn' was founded, a Saxon village, one of the four little places from which modern Eastbourne grew. Until the mid 19th century they were separated by cornfields and elm-fringed lanes. Old Eastbourne **9** lies a mile inland from the coast, a distinct and special part of the town. It clusters around the large flint and stone Norman

15

Long Man of Wilmington

the name is Norman French) lends its own special flavour to the seaward end of the Wealdway, for its aura hangs over the great whale-backed down of which it is a part. From the downs **14** Eastbourne and its environs are spread out in a panorama, backed by the curving sweep of the coast

Jevington church

around Pevensey Bay where the Weald reaches the sea.

Just over a mile (1.6km) to west of the lighthouse, stands another lighthouse, on Belle Tout. Being only 30 feet (9.1m) from the eroding cliff face, engineers, in 1999, moved the whole building back 56 feet (17m) to a safer site.

Antiquities of the South Downs

Several thousand years of human handiwork are visible in the Southdown landscape. The oldest date from neolithic

times. Of these the most spectacular is the causewayed camp which crowns Combe Hill **18**, one of six such camps on the South Downs. They are intriguing because the concentric ditches that surround them are broken, the undisturbed ground forming 'causeways'. At Combe Hill at least 16 causeways have been recorded. These camps probably ended up as hilltop settlements, as indeed were similar camps on the Continent, but may have been ceremonial and ritual enclosures and possibly served as market places where goods and cattle were exchanged. The Combe Hill camp was in use in about 3400BC.

On Windover Hill, Wilmington, to the south and east of the enigmatic Long Man **26** are a group of neolithic flint mines, dating from about 3000BC. They are

marked today by a series of humps and hollows. Also of neolithic age are long barrows (elongated earthen burial mounds), including Hunter's Burgh **25**.

Younger than these antiquities are the many Bronze Age and later round barrows (tumuli) which tend to stand along the skyline. There is an Iron Age promontory fort at Belle Tout, the coastal down between Beachy Head and Birling Gap.

Most of the once numerous Celtic field systems of the downs have been destroyed by modern agriculture and in East Sussex the best remaining are on Combe Hill near Jevington **19** and Windover Hill. These small ancient fields – probably mostly Iron Age and Romano-British – are bounded by banks and tend to be found on south-facing slopes.

There are numerous downland trackways of unknown age. Many are probably prehistoric, of which the best known is the South Downs ridgeway which was a major route by the Bronze Age and perhaps earlier. The steep northern slopes of the downs

are descended by terraceways. An excellent terraceway, on a continuous gradient, descends Wilmington Hill to the east of the Long Man. It is covered by short springy turf, such as is found on ancient roadways, and is very likely of Roman age. Uphill it joins up with an old coach road which had come up from the Cuckmere valley at Milton Street **30**. Above the Long Man this narrow trackway has been given the name of the 'Giants Causeway', and some people believe it too is Roman.

Jevington

Jevington **20**, hidden among the enfolding South Downs, is a small village with a long history. The cottage architecture is typical of the downland region, with plenty of flint and timber and some hung tiles, and all on a scale in harmony with the surrounding landscape.

The Romans were at Jevington and their road linking this downland spot to the outside world came up from the Weald at Willingdon and crossed Helling Down to arrive here at Street Farm **22**.

The church, dedicated to St Andrew **21** and standing a little above the village, is probably on an ancient site. The tower is Saxon and contains re-used Roman bricks. There is other Saxon work here, a wonderfully moving sculpture, found during church restoration. It now resides in the north wall of the nave and shows Christ killing the serpent with a sword.

Opposite the church is 'Monastery Field', thought to be the site of the 14th-century monastery of St Lewina, the first Sussex martyr.

Jevington's location made it a particular resort of smugglers during the 18th century, since contraband could easily find its way here from its coastal landing places. Legends are plentiful about the secret passages and hidden vaults under the apparently innocent cottages that still line the village street. One of the most notorious of all Sussex smugglers, Jevington Jigg, was a native of Jevington, and once lived at the present Hungry Monk restaurant. The law was constantly after him but for years he evaded

capture, once by dressing in women's clothes and pretending to have the hysterics, but in the end he was apprehended and convicted of horse stealing. In 1799 he was transported to Botany Bay where he is thought to have died.

Folkington

Folkington 23 – the old Sussex dialect would pronounce it 'Fowing-ton' – is hidden from the prying eyes of the world on a no-through road that ends under the downs. The little hamlet is canopied by venerable trees, and even walkers on the Wealdway, grown accustomed to reaching places by the back door, might pass it by without realising what a gem of tranquillity nestles here. The whole place has the air of having been

forgotten by the modern world. The church of St Peter 24, could be the very original of Kipling's 'Little lost down churches', a tiny 13th-century building of local flint, calm in its simplicity, restored by the Victorians and again in 1961. Inside are three large oaken box pews and an intriguing inscription to Catherine Thomas "a widow before she died" aged only 23.

Yet Folkington has had its fame. It was the home of Nicholas Culpepper (1616-54), the astrologer and medical writer whose famous 'Herball' is still in print. After Culpepper's time the hamlet was important for the growing of teasels which were used for dressing broadcloth.

The hanging woods, or 'hangers' at Folkington are rare on the downs of East Sussex, and provide a good habitat for woodland plants and animals. The badger setts in these very woods prompted the introduction of the Badger Protection Act into the House of Lords in the 1960s.

The Long Man of Wilmington

Windover Hill – 'Windoor Hill' on the old maps – is known the world over for the 230-

foot (71m) high chalk-cut figure of The Long Man 26, the largest representation of the human form in Europe. Yet he is a strange being, for no one knows who put him there or why, and his makers are quoted variously as Celts, Romans, Vikings, Saxons, and the monks of Wilmington Priory. He has been skilfully drawn so as not to appear foreshortened from below. From the present car park in Wilmington, if you disregard the positions of his feet, the giant appears to be stepping straight out of the hillside towards you.

The earliest known drawing of him dates from 1710, and 'Longman Lane' (proving that this has been his local name for centuries) gets a mention in estate records of 1765. He was described in 1781 with an accompanying drawing making him look like a bandy-legged yokel, complete with honest face and long-handled rake and scythe. By 1807 his face was featureless and he had lost his agricultural implements, bearing instead two staves. In 1835 Horsfield wrote in his 'History and Topography of the County of Sussex' that "the lower parts are at all times extremely indistinct". This was probably because of the downhill movement of soil filling in the shallow trench that demarked him. He was rescued from oblivion in 1874 by the Revd de Ste Croix who had him outlined in white bricks, and it was at this stage

On the downs near Folkington

17

Cottage at Wilmington

18

century and the nave 14th century with a 13th-century north chapel containing a stained glass window showing St Peter surrounded by bees and butterflies, some of them only found in Sussex. In the chancel is a Norman carving of a seated figure, possibly the virgin and child. Strange

that he was given feet pointing eastwards – like the Cerne Abbas giant. The bricks were replaced by concrete blocks in 1969, perpetuating the Victorian interpretation.

But who is he? Odin? or Baldur, the Norse god of Spring, opening the gates of the dawn? Is he a fertility symbol like the Cerne Abbas giant? Is he Hercules or is he there to guide pilgrims to Wilmington Priory? The Long Man keeps his secret still, staring blankly northwards over the Weald, teasing us with our inability to fathom him.

Wilmington

Wilmington 27, the name is Saxon, is an attractive village of well-kept cottages strung along a lane beneath the downs. And whatever doubts there

may be as to the antiquity of the Long Man there is one 'resident' in Wilmington that, if we are to believe modern science, goes back to the close of the Roman Empire. This is the great yew tree in the churchyard, which is now thought to be 1,600 years old. It must be about the oldest living thing in the British Isles.

The church, dedicated to St Mary and St Peter 29, was formerly the priory church and stands close by the ruins of the Benedictine priory. The present church, with its 'Sussex cap' and squat tower, is much younger than the yew tree, the chancel is 12th

Overlooking Arlington, at Parkwood Farm

to think that the yew tree, with its massive props and confining chains was already several centuries old when this carving was new.

Wilmington Priory 28 was established in 1088, and belonged to the Benedictine Abbey of Grestain in

Normandy. It was suppressed in 1414. Its ruins, some of which date from 1243, are incorporated into a private house. They formerly housed an agricultural museum. At the time of writing the priory is closed and breathes an air of neglect and uncertainty.

Cuckmere valley

Away to the west of the Wealdway the Cuckmere River flows into the sea at Cuckmere Haven, the only undeveloped river mouth in south-east England. The Wealdway nudges into the wide green valley some five miles inland, just north of the river gap through the downs at Milton Street 30. This name suggests a Roman road hereabouts. Howsoever that may be, Milton Street possessed a medieval castle which guarded the pass through the hills. All that remains is a great mound, 'Burlough Castle'.

Alfriston (TQ 521032) is the best known Cuckmere village with plenty of old houses including the Clergy House (TQ 522029) and the Star Inn. The red-painted figurehead outside the 'Star' came from a Dutch warship wrecked off Cuckmere Haven in the 1670s. Somehow one cannot help thinking of Sussex wreckers when one

looks at it. Alfriston's Market Cross (TQ 521032) is merely a stump, itself rebuilt after an argument with a lorry in 1955. This is one of only two market crosses surviving in Sussex, the other is the grand affair in central Chichester. Nearby stands another old inn, the 'Market Cross', with its other name, 'The Smugglers', betraying Alfriston's shady past. The church of St Andrew (TQ 522030), built in 1360, has a raised circular churchyard, suggesting it was built on a prehistoric barrow.

Farne Street and Endlewick

Just south of Arlington a trackway, known for centuries as Farne Street 33, runs along the Roman road to the fort at Pevensey. Called the 'old road' in a charter of 1252 it continued in use well into the coaching era. The Wealdway crosses Farne Street at Endlewick 32, a deserted medieval hamlet where Roman occupation is known.

Arlington

Arlington 35 is a gloriously secluded village on a dry site above the Cuckmere River. It seems like a place that time has forsaken. Yet time reigns here, for the flint-built Saxon church of St Pancras 36, once thought to stand above a Roman building, contains reused Roman bricks and tiles. The graceful spire was damaged by the Great Storm in 1987 but is now repaired 🜨

chapter 2

The Secret Weald

Upper Dicker to Buxted Park

> *Out of the Weald, the secret Weald*
> *Men brought in ancient years*
> *The horseshoes red at Flodden Field*
> *The arrows of Poitiers…*
> Kipling

20

Between the rolling chalk downland and the sandstone tracts of the High Weald lie the clay lowlands, the lands of the Weald Clay. This tough tenacious substance is hugely successful in growing trees (Repton commented that "every berry soon becomes a bush and every bush a tree") and the production of timber and timber products including charcoal, and for the making of bricks, pipes and clay pots. Buildings are half-timbered or weather-boarded, or made of local brick and tiles dug from the local clay: the houses at East Hoathly are fine examples. This is intense, inward-looking countryside, secretive and enclosed, where the burgeoning hedgerows are the direct descendants of the ancient forest of Andredsweald and the fields were hewn from the woodland at the expense of some 20 generations of sweat and toil. The wet clay soils seem themselves to echo the old Sussex saying "We won't be druv".

Highlands

Hellingly village

Charcoal and Iron

Mining and smelting of the iron-rich deposits of the Weald took place from before Roman times, the industry was mentioned by Caesar, down to the early days of the 19th century. The Weald was the Romans' 'Black Country', and after centuries of neglect became so again in the Middle Ages and Tudor times. The furnaces were fuelled by charcoal rather than coal, so the industry died when the process could be done more cheaply by the coal-fired furnaces of Derbyshire.

The 'ironstone' worked is a low-grade iron ore, mostly siderite, a clay ironstone which is found in most parts of the Weald. The iron industry is associated in particular with the High Weald but there are sites on the Weald Clay. There are many clues left in the landscape as to its whereabouts: names like Forge Wood, Gun Hill **48** and Minepit Shaw; hummocky ground and slag and cinder along stream-courses, as well as the remains of the hammer ponds – some now beautiful sheets of water with trees coming down to their shores – a far cry from how they looked when new! Hammer ponds were needed to give a head of water to power the forge-hammers and later to power the blast furnaces introduced in Tudor times. Frequently the broken embankment or pond 'bay' is all that remains. Ordnance – cannon and shot – were the chief products, with a lucrative sideline in firebacks, railings and other iron goods.

Sussex Potteries

A traditional Sussex verse runs:

" *Sussex clay be good and strong*
  to serve 'ee long and well
  Be it bricks, pots or pipes
  or strong tankards for good ale."

The deserted sites of several important potteries lie along the Wealdway and others lie close at hand, though there is little at all left to see. The potteries of Lower Dicker and Uckfield were hugely important in their time, and 'Sussex ware' was produced at both. The Dicker Pottery did not shut until the 1950s. Jonathan Harmer of Heathfield (1762-1849) was known for the terracotta gravestone plaques, several of which are to be seen along Wealdway.

'Dicker Common'

The two villages, Upper and Lower Dicker stand above the Cuckmere River in a flat, damp region formerly known as 'The Dicker' or 'Dyker Waste', and later as 'Dicker Common', one of the wild marshy wastelands that persisted in the Weald until the end of the 17th century, on the edge of the Ripe-Chalvington Roman land settlement scheme.

The two villages are of greatly varying character.

Sunset near Michelham Priory

Upper Dicker **39**, through which the Wealdway passes, is rather a charming spot dominated by the red-brick buildings of St Bede's School **40**, former home of Sir Horatio Bottomley, one-time MP for the area who was jailed for fraud in 1922. It is rumoured that even the bricks were from government stock. Many of the cottages in the village were also built by the MP.

Holy Trinity Church **41** is set at an angle to the road. It was built in 1843 in Norman style, using flints from Alfriston.

Lower Dicker (TQ 565113), about a mile from the Weald-way, is scattered along the main road and was, until the 1950s, well known as a centre of the Wealden pottery industry using the Weald Clay. This pottery, working from the 18th century, made pipes, tiles and chimney pots, many of which went to supply Brighton and Eastbourne.

Michelham Priory **42**

This house of Augustinian canons was founded in 1229 and dissolved in 1537, during Henry VIII's great purge. It came into the ownership of the Sackville family. It is now owned by the Sussex Archaeological Society and open to the public. It has a superb 14th-century gatehouse. Exhibitions are now housed in the vaulted undercroft.

Hailsham (TQ 590095)

The Wealdway skirts this busy modern town with a long history. It was mentioned in Domesday, where it was known as 'Hamelsham'. Until the 1950s curfew was rung at 8pm daily. Hailsham has modern shopping arcades, a leisure complex (The Lagoon) and the Hailsham Heritage Centre. It lies on the Cuckoo Trail **43**, a leisure route on the line of the former Polegate-Heathfield railway originally known as the Cuckoo Line.

Horsebridge

Horsebridge is now little more than a suburb of Hailsham, and stands at an important bridging point of the Cuckmere River. Indeed, for years it was the lowest spot on the river where horse-drawn vehicles could cross dry-shod. The magnificent watermill **44**, its buildings now used by an engineering firm, was for generations a flour mill.

"Three lies and all true" – Hellingly, Chiddingly and East Hoathly

Many people in the clay Weald still speak in the soft tones of the old Sussex dialect, though even here the homely rural accent is sore pressed by modern uniformity of speech. In the Sussex dialect the final syllable is accented, so that Hellingly, for example, is pronounced Helling-lie, rather than Helling-lee. Thus, an old saying about the three adjacent villages of Hellingly, Chiddingly and East Hoathly: *"Three lies and all true"*! These villages all lie along the Wealdway to the north and west of Hailsham and all nestle as deep as can be in Sussex history.

Michelham Priory

23

Hellingly

Hellingly, with its tile-hung cottages of local baked clay, may indeed be best known for its former psychiatric hospital which served a large part of East Sussex and Kent but it is possibly very ancient indeed. It crowds around its raised circular churchyard – some seven feet (2.1m) above the village – and certainly an ancient 'cric' or burial ground. It probably pre-dates the Saxons, feeling back into Roman times and maybe earlier. The church **47** dates from Norman times, but its tower is much younger, built in 1836 to replace an earlier spire. It was extensively restored in 1869 at which time an ancient scratch-dial was reset upside down in a buttress. In the churchyard are terracotta plaques by Jonathan Harmer of Heathfield.

Hellingly has its place in legal history, for it was here in 1541 that Thomas Fiennes, Lord Dacre, murdered John Busby, gamekeeper to Sir Nicholas Pelham (that same Sir Nicholas who fought off the French at Seaford, and in whose memory Seaford beach is called 'The Pelham' to this day). Lord Dacre paid the penalty for his crime, dying on the scaffold, the first time in history that a nobleman was executed for killing a commoner.

Chiddingly

Chiddingly **49**, the second of these villages, is in size little more than a hamlet hidden in a maze of lanes between deep hedgerows, each with its intense shadow under summer sun and its mire and shade in winter. This is a village of warm brick walls, where there is still a village store and opposite, the Six Bells public house, a handsome building in chequered brick. It is all very traditional, very reassuring, and it is a delightful flight of fancy that once led to the place being compared to Rome, for Chiddingly, like the eternal city, is built on seven hills. On one of these hills stands the church **50** with its soaring spire, 130 feet (40m) tall. This is a stone spire, rare in Sussex where spires – if they are built at all – tend to be roofed in wooden shingles.

Chiddingly is celebrated as the former home of the Jeffray family. There were Jeffrays in the area at the time of the Wars of the Roses but the most famous of them, Sir John Jeffray, rose to be a Baron of the Exchequer under Elizabeth I, and died in 1578. Place Farm **52**, is a fragment of his home, Chiddingly Place, an imposing deep coloured brick house, its mullioned windows staring out over the centuries and calling to mind that the Jeffrays were said to be so proud that they walked to church each Sunday on cheeses placed before them like stepping stones, so that their feet would not touch the common ground. Possibly this myth arose from the massive Jeffray monument in the church, since the two upright figures stand on circular tablets. The monument has been somewhat 'knocked about', perhaps because the Jeffrays became confused in the public

Gun Inn, Gun Hill

mind with the notorious Judge Jeffries, who made his fortune by extortion during the 'Bloody Assizes'.

These people wrought in marble seem hardly to have lived or breathed, and certainly their voiceless effigies seem proud indeed! Yet, if ghostly tales are true, the Jeffrays were not all pride and hauteur but as capable of love and hate as the rest of us. Indeed, Sir Richard Milward, a knight of the 13th century, still walks the neighbourhood, and may be heard and seen on certain moonlit nights approaching with angry steps the nearby manor house of Pekes (TQ 554130), a home of the Jeffrays before they built Chiddingly Place. Here he gazes longingly at the house where Agnes, his beloved daughter, lived having eloped with John Jeffray, grandfather of Sir John, the baron.

East Hoathly

East Hoathly 53, last of the three "lies" of the area, is a pleasant brick and tile-hung village on a right-angled bend of the former A22 road. The village is now by-passed but the new road slashes through the parkland of the former mansion of the great Pelham family, Halland House, which was demolished at the end of the 18th century.

The Wealdway wanders through the old park 56 for a little space and although there is naught to see today, it is intriguing to contemplate the

vanished glory of the place. Halland House was built in 1595 when Sir Thomas Pelham moved his seat from nearby Laughton Park (TQ 502149). It was built in small bricks decorated with terracotta ornaments and sandstone and is thought to have resembled Kirby Hall in Northamptonshire. In later years a lime avenue was planted and the romantically minded may care to remember that lime or elm avenues were said to be planted according to whether the planter favoured the cause of William and Mary or the Jacobites.

East Hoathly church 55 was rebuilt in 1856 and is full of Pelham monuments, while the arms of the Pelhams (the famous Pelham buckle) stand over the west doorway. A real-life drama was enacted here in 1632 when Sir Thomas Lunsford, the 'Sussex

Hellingly church

Barn near Blackboys

Cannibal' attempted to murder his kinsman, Sir Thomas Pelham. The trace of the bullet was once said to have been visible in the west door, though no sign can be seen today. For this attack Lunsford was heavily fined. He was a morose and unpleasant character and had an unenviable reputation, being said to feed on children,

Buxted Park and Church of St Margaret

Detail of stained glass window in Church of St Margaret

later days it became a coaching inn. Charcoal-burning was the local industry here from the Middle Ages to the 18th century and probably gave the place its name. The place was known as 'Blakeboys' in 1437 but this may be a personal name since a Richard Blakeboy was recorded as living here in 1398. On the other hand, was he called Black-boy because he was a charcoal burner?

The tower of 1509 collapsed in 1667 and was not rebuilt until 1893. Some typically Wealden tiled and timber-framed cottages line the road leading to the church.

Framfield set a remarkable record in 1792 when the village assembled a cricket team of its oldest inhabitants with a combined age of over 1,000 years. They never played a match as they were unable to find a correspondingly Metheuselan team as opponents.

Uckfield

Uckfield, on the river Uck, is just off the Wealdway. It is an old established town on the edge of the High Weald with a myriad of modern suburbs and plenty of light industry. It was formerly an important centre both of the Wealden iron industry and later of the Sussex brick, tile and pottery industry. Today industries include pharmaceuticals and engineering.

The old part of the town stands at a T-junction where the High Street descends the hill towards the level crossing. The upper part of the High Street is mainly Georgian, with an attractive raised pavement, while the lower part is Victorian and Neo-Georgian. By the railway station stands Bridge Cottage (TQ 473208), one of the oldest buildings in Uckfield, a half-timbered Wealden hall house 🔄

keeping limbs in his pockets to sustain himself when he wanted a quick snack. He emigrated to Virginia in 1649.

An altogether more endearing denizen of East Hoathly was the diarist and chronicler of village life, Thomas Turner (1729-89). He earned his living as a wood and hop merchant and his house 54 still stands. His tales of high life at Halland

House, of drinking bouts and of tittle-tattle, make most enjoyable reading.

Blackboys 59

This village on the edge of the High Weald is known for the Blackboys Inn. In the 14th century this was a lonely alehouse set on the heights amid the activities of charcoal-burners producing fuel for the Wealden iron industry and in

Framfield (TQ 495204)

Church, inn and Framfield House lie on the west of this village which lies about a mile (1.6km) to the south-west of the Wealdway. The church of St Thomas Becket, which is reached up a brick path, was built in 1509 after fire destroyed an earlier church.

chapter 3

The Wilds of Ashdown Forest

Buxted Park to Summerford Farm

" *For pines are gossip pines the wide world through*
And full of runic tales to sigh or sing "
James Elroy Flecker

GRAVESEND

Borough
Green

Tonbridge

Royal
Tunbridge
Wells

Crowborough

Uckfield

Hailsham

EASTBOURNE

ASHDOWN FOREST, high, heathy and wild, with scrubland, woodland and landmark groups of pines, was once billed as 'Sussex's answer to Scotland'. It is a watershed of the Weald, a high ridge with superb views southwards over the Weald Clay lowlands to the South Downs. The highest point is Crowborough Beacon (735 feet, 224m), but some of the best views are from the little clump of pines that crown Camp Hill (650 feet, 198m). It is one of the last remnants of the ancient forest of Andredsweald, an untamed place for all that its northern margin is but 30 miles (48km) from London. Ashdown was wild and lawless during the 18th century when it was a favoured haunt of the 'gentlemen' – Sussex smugglers. For centuries Ashdown was an important centre of the Wealden iron industry but today it is known for its varied plants and wildlife.

The commons of Ashdown Forest

For three thousand or so years before the Romans, men had been making inroads into the ancient forest, felling the trees and creating clearings. The Romans felled large tracts of the surviving ancient forest and developed extensive iron works and tile works in the region. One of their important trade routes, the London–Lewes road, runs across Ashdown Forest and is followed in part by the Wealdway. This was used to transport iron from the Weald

Lepham's Bridge, near Uckfield

29

View from Camp Hill, Ashdown Forest

and corn grown on the South Downs towards the Thames and London. With the Romans' departure in the 5th century the trees and scrub overran their farmsteads and mines, fast becoming dense secondary woodland and developing into the great forest of Andredsweald.

The commons of Ashdown Forest developed during the Dark Ages when the Jutes of Kent and the Saxons of Sussex used the Andredsweald wilderness as common land for grazing cattle in summer and big herds of swine during the autumn – the latter fattened on beechmast and acorns. The summer grazing clearings were known as 'dens' and over the years became isolated farms. After the Norman conquest arable farming was developed in some of the clearings.

Ashdown was created a Royal Hunting Forest in 1268. Then Edward III gave it to John of Gaunt. It was heathland at the time it became a hunting forest. It passed into the hands of the Earls of Bristol and the Earls of Dorset, who enclosed parts of it. The word forest means an area where deer are enclosed, not an area of trees, as most perceive nowadays. The 'Forest men', commoners living in the Ashdown parishes, quite rightly saw the enclosures destroying their livelihoods and fought for over 40 years to preserve the forest as common land. The commoners' fight

culminated in the Decree of 1693, a compromise in which a larger acreage (6,400 acres, 2,590.02 hec) of common land was preserved and this was at the edges of the forest close to the forest settlements. For the next hundred years or so the enclosed land remained

plant trees for timber and build farms in some of the enclosures. A Board of Conservators was set up under the first Ashdown Forest Act of 1885 to manage the area. The forest is freely open to the public and there are many forest rides and

Ashdown's varied plants and wildlife

Ashdown Forest is part of the High Weald Area of Outstanding Natural Beauty (AONB), a Site of Special Scientific Interest (SSSI) and a Special Protected Area (SPA) on account of the range of

much as before, mostly as rabbit warrens (names such as Crowborough Warren survive) but in the 18th century people began to

footpaths. Military training took place here in the Second World War and the army still owns a training site in the centre of the original area.

plants, animals and birds to be found there. It is one of the few places in Sussex where marsh gentian flowers and some very rare butterflies are found. The largest mammals in the forest today are deer. Badgers are plentiful as are foxes, shrews and water voles. Bats are common, including the rare mouse-eared bat. These are the largest European bat and in Britain are resident only in Sussex. Among the reptiles are lizards, grass snakes and adders. The birdlife of Ashdown is prolific. Birds of prey include migrant hobbys and the winter visiting hen harriers. Other winter visitors include crossbills and siskins, while tree pipits, wood warblers and redstarts are among the summer migrants. Nightjars can still be heard on Ashdown, their low 'churring' song droning into the dark.

Iron working of the Ashdown Forest

Iron ores of the Weald are found on Ashdown Forest at the junction of the Wadhurst Clay and the Ashdown Sand. Mining took place principally in the steep-sided ghylls where the seams of ore could be more easily exploited. Remains of iron works are scattered over Ashdown Forest with overgrown and broken remnants from prehistoric, Roman, medieval and later times. Overgrown heaps of slag and cinder occur near the deserted sites. The minepits themselves are frequently visible. Early furnaces, from prehistoric to medieval, were of the bloomery type, but by the mid 15th century big

changes were afoot and the forge hammer was being employed, requiring a head of water to power it and leading to the damming of streams to provide it; the earliest known Sussex hammer was at Burwash in the 1430s. Later, the blast furnace was introduced, requiring even greater use of water power to work the bellows as well as the hammers. Newbridge, on the forest, is the first recorded blast furnace in England in 1498. In 1543, Ralph Hogge successfully cast cannon for the first time in England – it was already being done in France – and the Weald became the centre of English ordnance manufacture.

It is not known at which furnace the first cannon was cast and it is not certain that it was at Huggett's Furnace. It is possible that it may have been Hendall Furnace 71, which lies virtually on the Wealdway. This was owned by the Pelham family and later by the Pope family and the overgrown pond bay (embankment) can still be traced. Another contender for the casting of the first cannon is Oldlands Furnace 74 just to the east of the Wealdway which was owned and possibly worked by the famous Parson Levett.

Buxted Park and site of medieval village

The Wealdway zigzags across the spacious and beautiful deer park attached to Buxted

Cottages near Oldlands

Park 66, now an hotel and conference centre, which was rebuilt after a fire in 1940. The house was originally built in 1726 by Thomas Medley to replace the medieval manor house which he pulled down.

The church of St Margaret of Scotland 67, where Christopher Wordsworth, the poet's brother, was rector for 50 years, was built in the 13th century and has a curious

16th-century carving over the north porch, showing a figure turning a churn. This is a pun on the name of the Alchorn family who built the church. The elegant 17th-century plaster ceiling covers a 14th-century barrel roof. The church now stands alone in the park but until the 1830s it stood amid the village of Buxted 68. In order to provide his house with

Management of the heathland of Ashdown Forest

The Conservators are required by law to conserve the Forest as a quiet and natural area of outstanding beauty. It is their policy to conserve the Forest by keeping a balance between woodland and heathland.

The 4,000 acres (1618.76hec) of heathland on Ashdown Forest represents a significant proportion of the total remaining lowland heath in the country. It is part of one of the rarest and most threatened habitats in Europe and is home to many important animal and plant species, including nightjars, Dartford warblers, silver-studded blue butterflies, bog asphodels, insect-eating sundews, marsh gentians and three species of heather.

Origins of heathland

Lowland heath was created by Man thousands of years ago when he cleared the trees on poor sandy soil to allow farming. The heathland of Ashdown Forest was maintained by Commoners who grazed their cattle and sheep, cut firewood and bracken, and burnt areas to improve grazing.

In 1985, the last Commoner grazing large numbers withdrew his stock because of the number of sheep he was losing in road accidents.

Since then, despite major cutting programmes introduced with the support of the Countryside Commission Stewardship Schemes and English Nature, the heathland has deteriorated under the invasion of Scots pine and birch.

Managing the heath

In 1985 the Conservators, in conjunction with English Nature, commissioned Land Use Consultants to advise on the best methods of managing the heathland. The Consultants' advice was that grazing, supported by cutting and, where appropriate, burning would be the most effective solution.

Grazing trial

Acting on this advice the Conservators set up a 100-acre (40.47hec) grazing trial in 1989 in the Millbrook area. The trial showed that, by grazing, the invasion of the heathland by birch could be stopped.

It is primarily to control birch scrub that the Conservators subsequently increased the grazing in line with the land use consultants' recommendations.

The Wealdway skirts the eastern edge of the grazed area between Duddleswell crossroads and Kings Standing.

Hendall Woods

as suitably lovely parkland setting, Lord Liverpool moved his estate village to the north-east where it still stands enlarged by time and prosperity due to the coming of the railway. To the west and the north-east of the church are noticeable platforms in the close-cropped turf – the sites of the old cottages of the lost village.

Facing the main road stands Hogge House **69**, dated 1581, with a black painted carving of a hog above the door. This was reputedly once the home of the Hogge or Huggett family, probably the most famous of all the Sussex ironmasters, with Ralph Hogge at their head, the man of whom the rhyme was written:

" Master Huggett and his man John They did cast the first cannon".

Maresfield (TQ 466241)

Pleasant old-world Maresfield, with its tile-hung cottages and the well-known Georgian inn, 'The Chequers', lies just under a mile (1.6km) from the Wealdway. The great house, Maresfield Park, is now demolished, but its gatehouse still stands. Maresfield was an important centre of the Wealden iron industry and had three foundries. The last was converted into a powder mill but this too has now gone. The former hammer ponds (TQ 461229) are now wild and beautiful spots, growing with water lilies and supporting extensive bird life.

The Wealden iron industry is commemorated in the church of St Bartholomew (TQ 466240) by the iron tombstone to Robert Brookes (died 1667). Such tombstones occur throughout the old iron region, the most notable collection of them being at Wadhurst. The church itself was originally Norman with a 15th-century west tower but was somewhat brutally restored in 1875-79. One ancient window survives in the nave.

One curiosity at Maresfield is the cast iron milestone (TQ 466241), one of the 'Bow Bells' set and dating from the second half of the 18th century. It gives the distance to Bow Bells and is decorated with bells and the Pelham Buckle, the badge of the important local family. Such cast iron milestones were made in the local iron works.

Fairwarp

The village of Fairwarp 73 has grown up since 1777 though the name 'Fayre Warp' occurs as far back as 1519. It seems to have grown from a farmhouse later called Rose Cottage and by 1873 there were about 12 houses, leading to an infants school being opened here. A new parish was created in 1881, carved out of Buxted and Christ Church was built. This was enlarged in 1930 with money from the influential Eckstein family to whom there are monuments signed by

William Reid Dick. The church is floored with travertine and there is an interesting arrangement to the staircase in the tower.

Oldlands 74

Oldlands Wood appears as 'Eldelond' in a document of 1219, meaning 'the old lands' and is thought to relate to Roman iron workings here. Later Tudor iron works here were worked by Parson Levett, the famous partner of Ralph Hogge. The writer, Coventry Patmore, lived at Oldlands from 1866 to 1870. The present Oldlands Hall (not open to the public) was built in the 1870s by Alexander Nesbitt but the site is ancient.

Near Oldlands corner

Duddleswell

Duddleswell, an ancient and historic spot, is but a scatter of houses and farms on the B2026 road which here runs along the line of the Roman road from London to Lewes. Saxon coins were discovered at Duddleswell in 1820, the only evidence that the Saxons ever occupied Ashdown Forest. Duddleswell has always been a small group of farms and houses but during the Middle Ages, when it was one of the six walks of the old Ashdown deer forest, its manor was held directly by the king, that is it was a Royal Manor (at present it is owned by East Sussex County Council but formerly held by Earl de la

Warr before his demise).

Duddleswell Manor 76, which is venerable itself in that it dates from the 10th century, stands on the site of even earlier manor houses. Opposite are the forlorn remains of the old Dudeney Chapel 77, unearthed in 1855.

Camp Hill 80

Rising to 650 feet (198m) and crowned by a clump of pines – signal pines – Camp Hill is a recognisable landmark, named after a British Army encamped there in the 18th century, sent to the coast to combat smuggling. Commanding extensive views over the Weald to the South Downs, it is one of the highest parts of Ashdown Forest. Undoubtedly a deliberate choice of site for the nearby radio station, where once stood a dominating network of tall masts, serving the Foreign Office Diplomatic Wireless Service, keeping London and British Embassies worldwide in touch with each other. During the Second World War propaganda, as well as coded messages, was transmitted to Allied Agents in occupied territory, using the letter V in Morse Code for identification. Now, less intrusive on the landscape, just one short and solitary mast remains.

London–Lewes Roman Road 81

This Roman road is followed closely by the Wealday for

some length of the trek over Ashdown Forest. It was a commercial road linking the iron-producing region with the financial capital of the province and the port of Lewes.

Five Hundred Acre Wood 84

The Wealdway passes through this woodland which was enclosed following the 1693 decree and whose trees were planted in the 18th century. The many gracious groves of beech and oak were badly affected by the Great Storm of 1987, but Nature is healing her wounds and the raw scars are no longer so obvious.

Hartfield (TQ 478358)

This delightful village with its street of weatherboarded, half-timbered and tile-hung cottages and houses, all very Wealden in nature, is close to the Wealdway. Today it is associated with A A Milne; from 1925 he lived at Cotchford Farm (TQ 476345), just outside the village, and wrote 'Winnie-the-Pooh' there. All kinds of 'Pooh' memorabilia are for sale at a 400-year-old shop in Hartfield High Street called, appropriately enough, 'Pooh Corner' (TQ 477356). Tea and ice cream are served in 'Piglet's Parlour'.

Cotchford Farm, where Milne lived for so many years is on the site of old Wealden iron workings. In the grounds is the original 'Poohsticks Bridge' (TQ 481374) much frequented by visitors. It

Hartfield

spans a tributary of the River Medway and is close to the site of a pond bay for a now-dry hammerpond.

Hartfield's church of St Mary (TQ 479357) with its tall spire is basically 13th century. It is approached via a lychgate (TQ 479357) beneath what were once a pair of Tudor cottages. Only one is still standing, the place of the other is taken by a yew tree.

Just north of the village stands Bolebrooke (TQ 481374), the remains of a large Tudor house which once belonged to the Dalyngrigges and later to the Sackvilles.

Withyham 88

This pleasant hamlet is connected with the Sackville family, many of whom including the poet Victoria Sackville-West (died 1962), are buried in its church. A cluster of quaint tile-hung houses of which the earliest, timber-framed 'Duckings' 89 , dated 1507, is close to an old hammerpond and is thought to have belonged to an iron master. Out of sight from the Wealdway but only a short walk from the church stands the elegant public house, the Dorset Arms, named after the Sackvilles, the Earls and later the Dukes of Dorset.

The church, St Michael and All Angels 90 , is up a steep lane outside the village. It had to be completely rebuilt after a lightning strike in 1663. An eyewitness reported that the lightning "came in at the steeple, melted the bells, and went up the chancel where it tore the monuments of the Dorsets in pieces". The sundial over the rebuilt porch is dated 1672, while the Sackville Chapel was completed in 1680. This chapel was built to house Caius Gabriel Cibber's magnificent monument to 13-year-old Thomas Sackville who had died in 1677. The tomb chest in grey and white marble is surmounted by an effigy of the boy holding a skull and flanked by life-size statues of his kneeling parents, the 5th Earl and Countess of Dorset. Other monuments in the chapel include a large tablet by Nollekens commemorating John Frederick, the 3rd Duke (died 1802); a wall plaque by Chantrey to Arabella, wife of the 3rd Duke (died 1825); a large tablet with a portrait medallion by Flaxman to the 4th Duke (died 1815) and a simple slate plaque by Reynolds Stone to Victoria Sackville-West.

Buckhurst Park 86 , home of the De La Warrs, a branch of the Sackville family, replaced Old Buckhurst which had belonged to the Sackvilles since the 13th century and of which only the restored 15th-century gatehouse now remains. It is not open to the public

Medway
Meadows

Summerford Farm
to Barnes Street

"When Kentish roads were few and bad,
Medway was the great highway…"
A Austin

Wealdway *questionnaire*

In order to help us assess the success of the Wealdway, we would like to hear from you about the route and the guidebook.

Please would you complete the questionnaire below and send it to the Environmental Management Unit, Strategic Planning Directorate, Invicta House, County Hall, Maidstone, Kent, ME14 1XX. If you have borrowed this book from a library or friend, you may photocopy the questionnaire.

1 Which of these statements best describes you?

I live close to the Wealdway ☐

I came to this area of East Sussex and Kent specifically to walk the Wealdway ☐

I did not came to this area of East Sussex and Kent specifically to walk the Wealdway ☐

2 Name of the country, or the town/village in the UK where you live (include the postcode)

....
....
....

3 How did you first become aware of the Wealdway?

Leaflet (which one)

....
....
....

Word-of-mouth ☐

Saw sign or waymark ☐

Newspaper (which one)

....
....
....

Other (write in)

....
....
....

4 What influenced you to try the Wealdway? (Tick more than one if applicable)

Countryside scenery ☐

Peace and quiet ☐

Local countryside nearby ☐

Interest in the area ☐

New area to explore ☐

New walk to try ☐

Wealdway guidebook ☐

Accessibilty (public transport) ☐

Promotional/ publicity material ☐

Other (write in)

....
....
....
....

5 Have you, or do you intend to:

Walk all of the route in one go over a short period of time (e.g. one week) ☐

Walk all of the route, in sections, over a longer period of time ☐

Walk only sections of the route ☐

Unlikely to walk any part of the route ☐

6 Which of the following modes of transport do you use to get to the start of your walk?

Walk ☐

Bus ☐

Cycle ☐

Train ☐

Car ☐

Other (write in)

....
....

7a Please indicate the age bracket of the person who bought this guidebook:

Age	Male	Female
Under 11	☐	☐
11–16	☐	☐
17–25	☐	☐
26–35	☐	☐
36–45	☐	☐
46–55	☐	☐
56–65	☐	☐
Over 65	☐	☐
Haven't done the walk yet		☐

7b How many people accompanied you on your walk? ☐

8 If you or your companions spent money on/in any of the following facilities/services in the area as a result of your walk, please indicate approximately how much in total (all group members).

Accommodation
£ ....

Food and drink in pubs £ ....

Food and drink from shops £ ....

Newspapers, gifts, souvenirs £ ....

Petrol £ ....

Clothing/equipment £ ....

Admission fees £ ....

Car parking £ ....

Others (write in)

.... £ ....

.... £ ....

.... £ ....

.... £ ....

9 Would you recommend the Wealdway to anyone else?

Yes ☐

No ☐

If you answered "no" please tell us why:

....
....
....

10 Where did you obtain this guidebook from?

Bookshop ☐

Chain store (e.g. WHSmith) ☐

Other shop (write in)

....
....

Tourist information centre ☐

Library ☐

Mail order ☐

11a What do you like about the guidebook?

....
....
....
....
....
....

11b What do you dislike about the guidebook?

....
....
....
....
....
....

12 How useful did you find the detachable route maps?

Very useful ☐

Useful ☐

Not useful ☐

Don't know ☐

13 Have you walked any section of these other routes?

North Downs Way ☐

South Downs Way ☐

Saxon Shore Way ☐

Greensand Way ☐

Royal Military Canal Path ☐

Darent Valley Path ☐

Stour Valley Walk ☐

Elham Valley Way ☐

Medway Valley Walk ☐

Eden Valley Walk ☐

High Weald Walk ☐

14 Are you a member of any of the following organisations? (Please tick boxes)

Ramblers' Association ☐

National Trust ☐

RSPB ☐

Wildlife Trust ☐

Other walking or countryside organisations (write in)

....
....

15 Are you a reader of any of the following publications for walkers?

The Great Outdoors ☐

Trail ☐

Country Walking ☐

Rambling Today ☐

South Eastern Rambler ☐

Other (write in)

....
....
....

A countryside journey across the Downs
and Weald of East Sussex and Kent

Along and *Around* the
Wealdway

Eastbourne ♦ Uckfield ♦ Tonbridge ♦ Gravesend

Walk guide

Includes Footpath Maps and
Ordnance Survey Maps

Wealdway

ESCC & KCC

Walk Guide Contents

Route map information

Wealdway The walk and its interesting features

Cover illustration: Ashdown Forest

Route map information

Route maps

THE ROUTE MAPS are reproduced from the Ordnance Survey Explorer series enlarged to an approximate scale of 3¼ inches to 1 mile (5.23cm to 1km).

The maps are aligned north/south on each page and the scale appears on each map spread.

The route has a 10mm repeat at the edge as you turn from page to page.

All sections of the walk follow legally defined rights of way unless otherwise indicated on route maps. Before using the guide, you are advised to study the key to the route maps and map symbols on page 3.

Each route map has an information box containing the following details:
- Route map number
- Starting and finishing places with Ordnance Survey grid references
- Distance and time
- Grading

Route directions

BECAUSE the countryside is constantly changing, with stiles and gates, and field boundaries being removed or new ones erected, there are no route directions in this guide. Route finding should not be a problem given the large-scale maps in the walk guide and the extensive waymarking on the ground.

Distances and times

THE DISTANCES and times for each sub-section of the route are shown on the map spreads.

The distances in this guidebook are given in miles. The exact conversion of miles to kilometres is 1 mile to 1.6093km. For convenience the approximate conversion is 1 mile to 1.6km.

Conversion table

1 mile	1.6km
2 miles	3.2km
5 miles	8km
10 miles	16.1km

Waymarking and signing

WAYMARKING The Wealdway waymarks are used to show the line of the route in the countryside. You will see them fixed to waymark posts, or posts of gates or stiles. The walk has been waymarked in such a way that it is possible to walk the route in either direction.

The route is waymarked by circular waymark discs with the letters WW in the centre

Waymarks

Sign post in Ashdown Forest

of the directional arrow. These are yellow on white for a public footpath, blue on white for a public bridleway and red on white for a public byway.

The exception is Ashdown Forest where short oak posts have indication arrows carved in the top.

See page 63 of the travel guide section for detailed information about the waymarking system.

Changes to the route may occur during the life of this guidebook, in which case look out for the diversion signs and follow the waymarks and signs.

SIGNING In East Sussex where the Wealdway crosses or leaves a metalled road there are oak fingerposts reading 'Wealdway' and either a walking person or horse symbol depending on the status of

East Sussex sign — WEALDWAY

the path. In Kent where the Wealdway crosses or leaves a metalled road there are metal signs fixed to lamp-posts or other posts. The logo is added to the footpath, bridleway or byway signs or used on its own where the route follows a section of road.

Grading system

Gradient

1	Level *up to 1 in 20*
2	Hilly but not too steep *up to 1 in 16*
3	Quite steep *up to 1 in 12*
4	Steep *up to 1 in 8*
5	Very steep *over 1 in 8*

Surface quality

A	Compact hard surface
B	Smoothish *Compact earth/short, even grass*
C	Semi-rough *Worn grass, attention given to remove the worst rocks and tree roots, looser hard surface*
D	Rough *Occasional ruts and stones or long grass*
E	Very rough *Lots of ruts and stones or loose gravel/hard surface*

Example

1A	This grade means that the length is fairly level and has a good hard surface

Please note the grades used are based on dry conditions and may be affected in bad weather.

1

◀ Footpath

Kent sign

Key to route maps and symbols
Ordnance Survey map symbols

Roads and paths

══════	Motorway
──────	Main road
──────	Secondary road
──────	Unclassified road
──────	Other road, drive or track

Unfenced roads and tracks are
shown by pecked lines

| - - - - - | Path |

Railways

──────	Multiple track
─illii─	Cutting
─illii─	Embankment
─·····─	Tunnel
─	Road over and under
─	Level crossing and station

Boundaries

— · — · — · —	County
— — — —	District
··········	Civil parish

Features

♠	Church or chapel with tower
♦	Church or chapel with spire
+	Church or chapel without tower or spire
▦	Glasshouse
△	Youth hostel
Ⱥ	Lighthouse
Λ	Beacon
△	Triangulation pillar
○ BP, BS	Boundary post/stone
℘	Public telephone
· MP, MS	Mile post/stone
	Gravel pit
	Sand pit
	Chalk pit, clay pit or quarry
	Refuse or slag heap
⊺⊺⊺⊺⊺⊺⊺⊺	Slopes
pylon pole	Electricity transmission line
○ W, Spr	Well, spring
	Sand, sand & shingle

Archaeological and historical sites

VILLA	Roman antiquity
Castle	Other antiquities
⚭	Site of antiquity
⚔ 1066	Site of battle (with date)

Vegetation

	Coniferous trees
	Non-coniferous trees
	Coppice
	Orchard
	Scrub
	Bracken, rough grassland
	Heath
	Reeds
	Marsh
	Saltings

Heights

50 · Surface heights are to the nearest metre above mean sea level.

Contours are not shown

Key to route maps

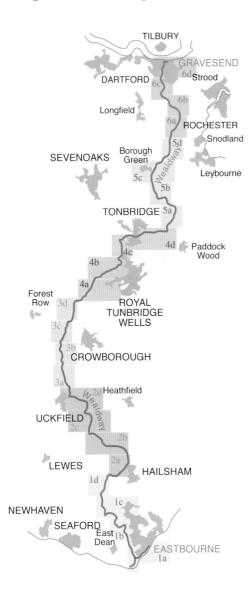

Route map symbols

——— Wealdway - fully signed and waymarked

— · — Alternative route - fully signed and waymarked.

— · · Optional access or detour – not signed or waymarked.

· · · · · Other footpaths – not promoted

[12] Interesting feature

(3) Miles from Eastbourne

page 16 Route map continuation

55e Right of way number

(59) Ordnance Survey grid number

River

Sea, pond or lake

Country park

Railway station

Bus route

P Car parking

Telephone

Post office

i Tourist information

WC Toilet

Accommodation

yha Youth hostel

Public house

Pub food

Café/restaurant

Refreshments

Picnic site

Foodstore

Viewpoint

Caution - take care

3

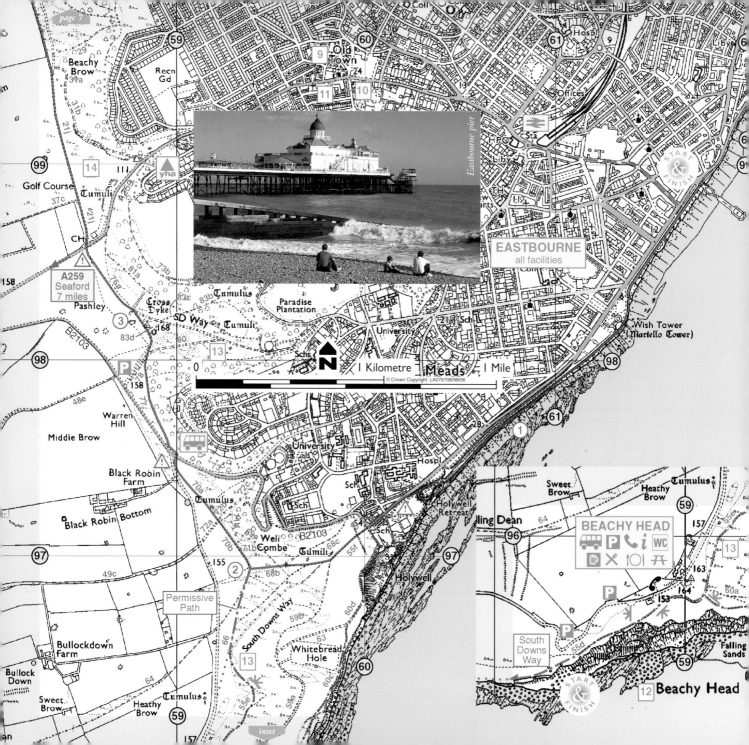

Eastbourne pier

EASTBOURNE
all facilities

Beachy Brow
34a
Recn Gd
Old Town
Offices
Sta

Golf Course
Tumuli
yha
A259
Seaford
7 miles
Pashley
Cross Dyke
SD Way
Tumuli
Tumulus
Paradise Plantation
University
Wish Tower
(Martello Tower)
Schs

0 | Kilometre | Mile
© Crown Copyright. LA076708/98/06

Meads
158
Warren Hill
Middle Brow
Black Robin Farm
Black Robin Bottom
Tumulus
University
Hospl
Holywell Retreat
B2103
Well Combe
Tumuli
Holywell
Bullockdown Farm
Permissive Path
Bullock Down
Sweet Brow
Heathy Brow
Tumulus
South Downs Way
Whitebread Hole
Sweet Brow
Heathy Brow

lling Dean
Falling Dean

BEACHY HEAD
WC

157
163
164
60a
153
South Downs Way
Falling Sands
Beachy Head

START & FINISH
inset

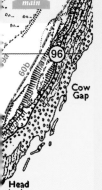

The Redoubt

Wealdway ~ *The walk and its interesting features*

The Downs *and the* Sea

Eastbourne or Beachy Head to Upper Dicker

Map 1a

Eastbourne (TV 618989) — *Beachy Brow* (TV 583996)
4 miles (6.4km), allow 2 hours   *Grade 2/5 B*

THE SOUTH DOWNS, the chalk hills which form the southern rim of the Weald and plunge to the English Channel at Beachy Head (533 feet, 164m), are an open, treeless landscape of uplands and little valleys, fanned by bracing sea winds. Today they are largely given over to arable fields and the big flocks of Southdown sheep which grazed them until the Second World War have been evicted by the plough. The handiwork of humanity is written large here and the history correspondingly long. There are prehistoric monuments, numerous ancient trackways, the enigmatic Long Man of Wilmington, flint-built churches of Saxon age and little hamlets and villages. Eastbourne, the spacious south coast resort, is a fitting beginning or end to the Wealdway, cradled in the lee of Beachy Head where the downs reach the sea.

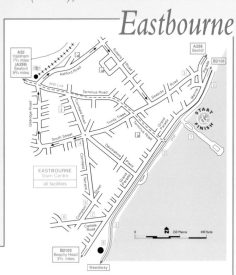

Eastbourne

5

Interesting features

SOVEREIGN HARBOUR
(TQ 642017)
A new marina complex with two docks, giving Eastbourne a proper harbour rather than boats having to beach on the shore.

MUSGRAVE COLLECTION
(TV 625999)
Paintings, sculptures, Roman and British coins, Roman and Egyptian artefacts and historical documents are displayed here.

BUTTERFLY CENTRE (TV 625999)
An undercover tropical garden, providing the perfect habitat for hundreds of exotic butterflies.

REDOUBT FORTRESS (TV 623997)
Built in 1804-1812, when Britain was threatened with a French invasion, it now houses the largest military museum in the South East.

1 EASTBOURNE PIER
The Victorian pier, which has a range of

entertainment, was built 1866-72.

2 EASTBOURNE PROMENADE
The three-tiered promenade is famous for its internationally-acclaimed 'Carpet Gardens'. Concerts are held at the Victorian bandstand. 'Dotto Trains' ply along the 'prom'.

3 ROYAL HIPPODROME
Traditional seaside variety is offered at

Eastbourne's oldest theatre throughout the summer season.

4 MUSEUM OF SHOPS
Three floors of authentic Victorian-style shops and rooms with over a hundred thousand exhibits. The wartime displays are particularly fascinating.

5 DEVONSHIRE PARK THEATRE
A Victorian theatre which puts on classic drama with leading screen and stage stars.

6

6 CONGRESS THEATRE
At Eastbourne's main theatre, top productions of ballet, musicals and comedy are staged throughout the year.

7 EASTBOURNE HERITAGE CENTRE
Charting the story of Eastbourne, there are award-winning displays including Eastbourne's royal connections, famous Eastbourne people, the railway and Beachy Head.

8 WISH TOWER AND RNLI LIFEBOAT MUSEUM
The Wish Tower is Martello tower number 73, one of over a hundred gun stations built at the time of the threatened Napoleonic Invasion. It houses an exhibition about the towers. Beneath it is the RNLI Lifeboat Museum, tracing the history of Eastbourne's lifeboats from 1853.

9 EASTBOURNE OLD TOWN
Originally the Saxon village of Bourn, from which Eastbourne developed towards the sea. The old town is about a mile (1.6km) inland and is clustered around the Towner Museum, St Mary's Church and 'The Lamb', which has been a hostelry since the 13th century.

10 TOWNER MUSEUM AND ART GALLERY
The Towner Art Gallery and Local Museum, built in 1770, is the former manor house of the Gilberts. There is an excellent collection of 19th and 20th-century art, with exhibitions throughout the year.

11 CHURCH OF ST MARY
The spiritual centre of the old town, with a fine Norman tower. In the churchyard is a Norman cross, from St Erth in Cornwall, together with the old village cross, now a sundial.

12 BEACHY HEAD
Beachy Head, the highest cliff on the south coast, rises 536 feet (164m) from the sea. There are spectacular views from the headland and the line of chalk cliffs that extend westwards to Brighton.

13 SOUTH DOWNS WAY
The famous National Trail, running for 101 miles (161.6m) along the South Downs from Eastbourne to Winchester. At the eastern end there are two routes, an inland bridleway and a coastal path.

14 EASTBOURNE DOWNLAND
The four thousand acres (1,618.76hec) of downland bordering the town was purchased in the 1920s in order to prevent further development. It is a haven for traditional downland grass and flowers. Sheep, have been reintroduced to help preserve this ancient landscape.

Map 1b
Beachy Brow (TV 583996) −
Cranedown Bottom (TQ 562030)
4 miles (6.4km), allow 2 hours Grade 3 D/E

Interesting features

15 MEMORIAL TO UNITED STATES AIRMEN
Overlooking Eastbourne is a memorial tablet to ten US airmen who died in 1944 when their Liberator bomber crashed into the hillside. They were returning to base, badly damaged, but hit the hillside on a foggy morning.

TUMULI
There are very large numbers of round burial mounds on the downs dating from the Bronze Age (about 2000BC) onwards to Saxon times.

16 BABYLON DOWN
Babylon Down affords panoramic views over Eastbourne, the wide Pevensey Levels and along the coast towards Hastings and Dungeness. Inland, the wooded Weald can be seen.

17 BUTTS LANE
The lane was once part of a road over the downs to Friston but now reduced in size to a bridleway. It makes a precipitous descent into Willingdon.

18 COMBE HILL NEOLITHIC CAUSEWAYED CAMP
This neolithic causewayed camp, dating from about 3400BC, is one of six on the South Downs. It may have originally been a ceremonial and ritual enclosure but its last use was as a settlement.

19 CELTIC FIELD SYSTEM, NEAR JEVINGTON
There were formerly many Celtic (Iron Age) field

Beachy Head

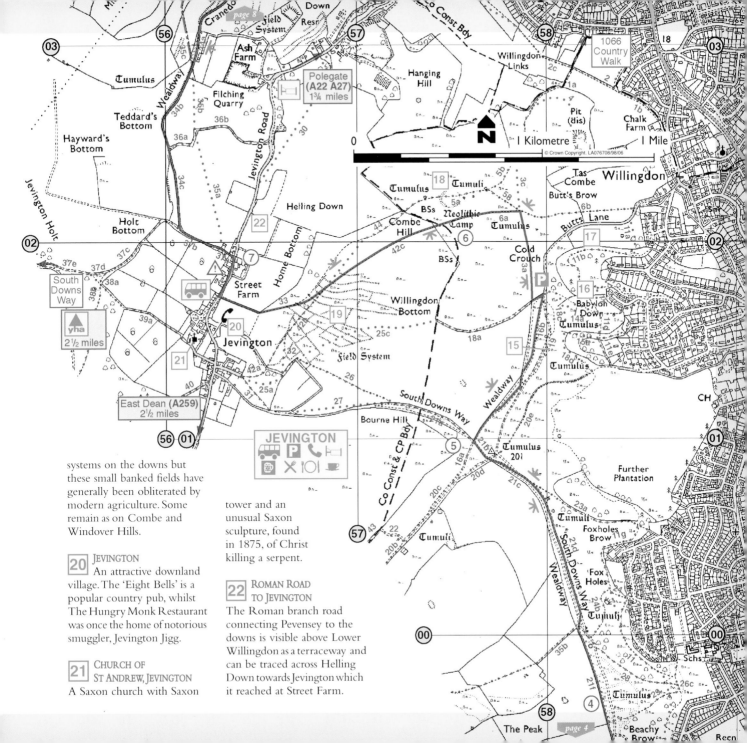

page 8

1066 Country Walk

© Crown Copyright. LA076708/98/06

0   I Kilometre   I Mile

Polegate (A22 A27) 1¾ miles

South Downs Way

yha 2½ miles

East Dean (A259) 2½ miles

JEVINGTON P

systems on the downs but these small banked fields have generally been obliterated by modern agriculture. Some remain as on Combe and Windover Hills.

20 JEVINGTON
An attractive downland village. The 'Eight Bells' is a popular country pub, whilst The Hungry Monk Restaurant was once the home of notorious smuggler, Jevington Jigg.

21 CHURCH OF ST ANDREW, JEVINGTON
A Saxon church with Saxon tower and an unusual Saxon sculpture, found in 1875, of Christ killing a serpent.

22 ROMAN ROAD TO JEVINGTON
The Roman branch road connecting Pevensey to the downs is visible above Lower Willingdon as a terraceway and can be traced across Helling Down towards Jevington which it reached at Street Farm.

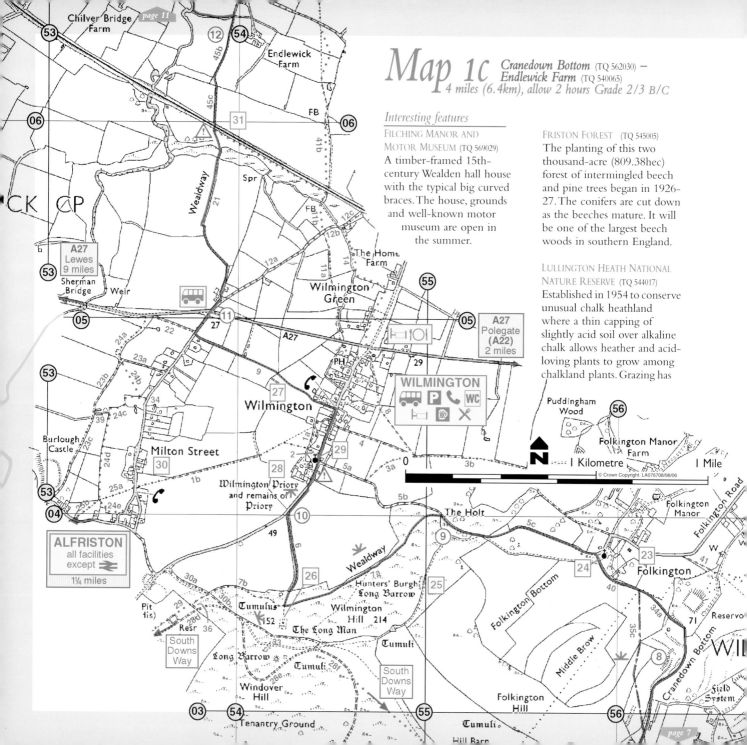

Map 1c

Cranedown Bottom (TQ 562030) –
Endlewick Farm (TQ 540065)
4 miles (6.4km), allow 2 hours Grade 2/3 B/C

Interesting features

FILCHING MANOR AND MOTOR MUSEUM (TQ 569029)
A timber-framed 15th-century Wealden hall house with the typical big curved braces. The house, grounds and well-known motor museum are open in the summer.

FRISTON FOREST (TQ 545005)
The planting of this two thousand-acre (809.38hec) forest of intermingled beech and pine trees began in 1926-27. The conifers are cut down as the beeches mature. It will be one of the largest beech woods in southern England.

LULLINGTON HEATH NATIONAL NATURE RESERVE (TQ 544017)
Established in 1954 to conserve unusual chalk heathland where a thin capping of slightly acid soil over alkaline chalk allows heather and acid-loving plants to grow among chalkland plants. Grazing has

© Crown Copyright. LA076708/98/06

been reintroduced to keep down scrub.

23 FOLKINGTON
This tiny hamlet, hidden in a downland hangar just touched by the Wealdway, lies less than a mile (1.6km) off the A27 road. It is a quiet, remote spot, bypassed by the modern world.

24 CHURCH OF ST PETER, FOLKINGTON
A simple flint-built downland church with a typical 'Sussex cap', a weatherboarded bell-turret. There are oak box pews and some quaint epitaphs.

25 HUNTER'S BURGH LONG BARROW
This neolithic burial mound lies about half way up Wilmington Hill. It is aligned north–south and is about 180 feet long, 70 feet across and about 6 feet high (55 x 21.5 x 1.8m). The side ditches are pronounced.

26 LONG MAN OF WILMINGTON
No one knows who cut this human figure on Windover Hill nor what was his purpose, although there are many theories. His brooding presence dominates this part of the walk.

27 WILMINGTON
An attractive collection of rose-garlanded flint cottages strung along the lane. The village green is near the A27 road and there are several hostelries.

28 WILMINGTON PRIORY
Established in 1080, with the present ruins dating from 1243, this Benedictine priory is situated in a splendid location looking directly towards the enigmatic Long Man. It is no longer open to the public.

29 CHURCH OF ST MARY AND ST PETER, WILMINGTON
Known for its 'butterfly window' and for the 1,600-year-old yew tree in the churchyard, this downland church was formerly attached to the now-ruined priory.

30 MILTON STREET
An earthen mound near the Cuckmere River is believed to be the remains of Burlough Castle, the medieval fortification that guarded the river gap through the South Downs.

31 LEWES TO EASTBOURNE RAILWAY
The line from Brighton to Bulverhythe near Hastings opened in June 1846, and the branch from Polegate to Eastbourne in May 1849. Now all trains run to Eastbourne and the Polegate to Stone Cross section is closed.

Alfriston

Nestling in the Cuckmere valley, this well-known tourist spot is regarded by many as the 'capital' of the downs. Its High Street has many fine Wealden buildings.

CLERGY HOUSE (TQ 522029)
This thatched and timbered Wealden house, built for the priests of the church in 1350, was the first property acquired by the National Trust, in 1896.

MARKET CROSS (TQ 521032)
At the north end of the village is the market cross, one of only two in Sussex. Only the stump now remains and this itself was rebuilt in 1955.

HERITAGE CENTRE AND BLACKSMITHS (TQ 522032)
The 15th-century forge is now a museum, showing Alfriston's history since Saxon times.

CHURCH OF ST ANDREW (TQ 522030)
Built in 1360 in the shape of a Greek cross. The churchyard is circular, betraying that the church is built upon a prehistoric barrow, a feature found in Sussex but rare elsewhere.

9

Giant yew, Wilmington churchyard

Map 1d
Endlewick Farm (TQ 540065) –
Upper Dicker (TQ 553099)
2¾ miles (4.4 km), allow 1½ hours   Grade 1 B/C

Interesting features

DRUSILLA'S ZOO AND CRAFT CENTRE (TQ 525049)
A popular children's zoo with shops, a garden centre, playground and miniature railway. Nearby is a wine cellar and cider museum, craft centre and small pottery.

32 ENDLEWICK
A farm and group of cottages are all there is to see of this scattered hamlet but once there was a medieval settlement here, now deserted and lost.

33 FARNE STREET ROMAN ROAD
A disused trackway marks the line of the Roman road to Pevensey, the great shore fort of Anderida. It was known as the 'old road' in 1252 and as 'Farne Street' in the coaching era.

34 ARLINGTON RESERVOIR
South of Arlington village, the reservoir, with its paths, nature trails and aquatic pursuits, was built in 1971. A particularly fine belt of woodland lies on the western side.

BERWICK STATION (TQ 527067)
The railway arrived in 1846, and a settlement grew around the station. The old-fashioned station, signalbox and crossing gates, are a reminder of a scene which was common throughout the British Isles until the early 1960s.

35 ARLINGTON
A little gem of a village at a junction of minor roads close to the Cuckmere River. The inn, church and houses cluster together, all that one imagines of a Wealden settlement.

36 CHURCH OF ST PANCRAS, ARLINGTON
A flint-built Saxon church a field or so from the Cuckmere River. Roman bricks are found in the walls and Roman tiles in a double-splayed window head.

37 THE 'YEW TREE', ARLINGTON
The comfortable modernised village pub makes a welcome point to stop for refreshment. It has a large garden and a restaurant.

38 CUCKMERE RIVER
A true Sussex river, rising in the county and flowing south to reach the sea at Cuckmere Haven, the only undeveloped river mouth in south-east England.

RIPE LAND SETTLEMENT (TQ 510101)
The area around Ripe and Chalvington was one of several areas set aside for veterans of the Roman army when they retired from their regiments. The grid-iron nature of the settlement can still be seen today in the field boundary and road systems.

10

Church of St Pancras, Arlington

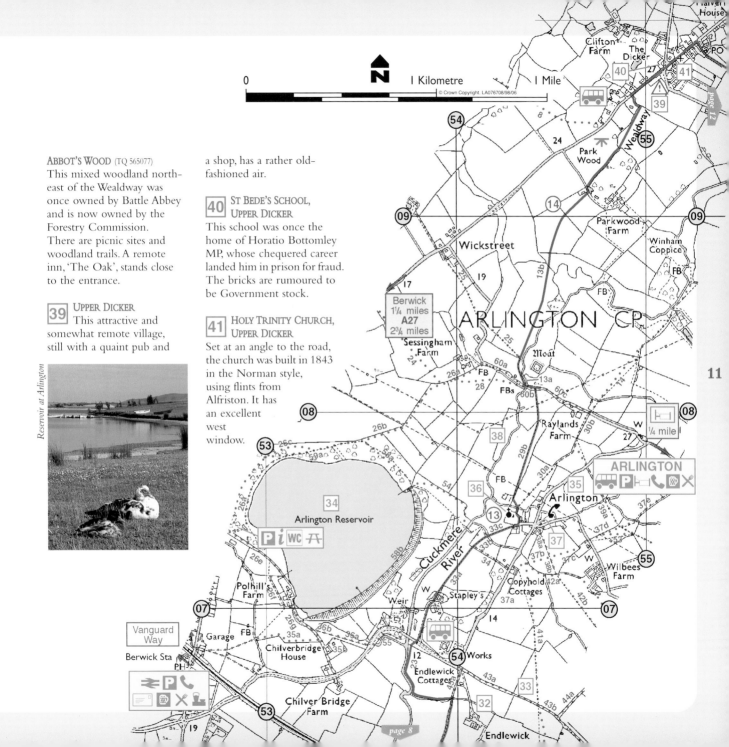

ABBOT'S WOOD (TQ 565077)
This mixed woodland north-east of the Wealdway was once owned by Battle Abbey and is now owned by the Forestry Commission. There are picnic sites and woodland trails. A remote inn, 'The Oak', stands close to the entrance.

39 UPPER DICKER
This attractive and somewhat remote village, still with a quaint pub and a shop, has a rather old-fashioned air.

40 ST BEDE'S SCHOOL, UPPER DICKER
This school was once the home of Horatio Bottomley MP, whose chequered career landed him in prison for fraud. The bricks are rumoured to be Government stock.

41 HOLY TRINITY CHURCH, UPPER DICKER
Set at an angle to the road, the church was built in 1843 in the Norman style, using flints from Alfriston. It has an excellent west window.

Reservoir at Arlington

11

page 12
page 8

The Secret Weald

Upper Dicker to Buxted Park

T HIS STRETCH OF THE WEALDWAY crosses the Vale of Sussex, low-lying clay land between the chalk downlands and the sandstone High Weald. The vale is still wooded, with the fields cut out of the forest. Wood was once much in demand for fuel and the making of charcoal to power local industries, including the famous Tudor ironworks. Weald Clay makes for a heavy, waterlogged soil and pastures predominate, grazed by herds of cattle. Arable land asserts itself as the land rises towards the sandstone heights. The roads were notorious, often impassable because of mud. The clay is good for tile and brick making, though these industries are less common than hitherto, when virtually every parish had its own brick-pit. The manufacture of clay and pots was once an important industry, notably at Lower Dicker. The local building materials were timber and fired clay and the Wealdway passes many magnificent half-timbered, tile-hung and brick houses.

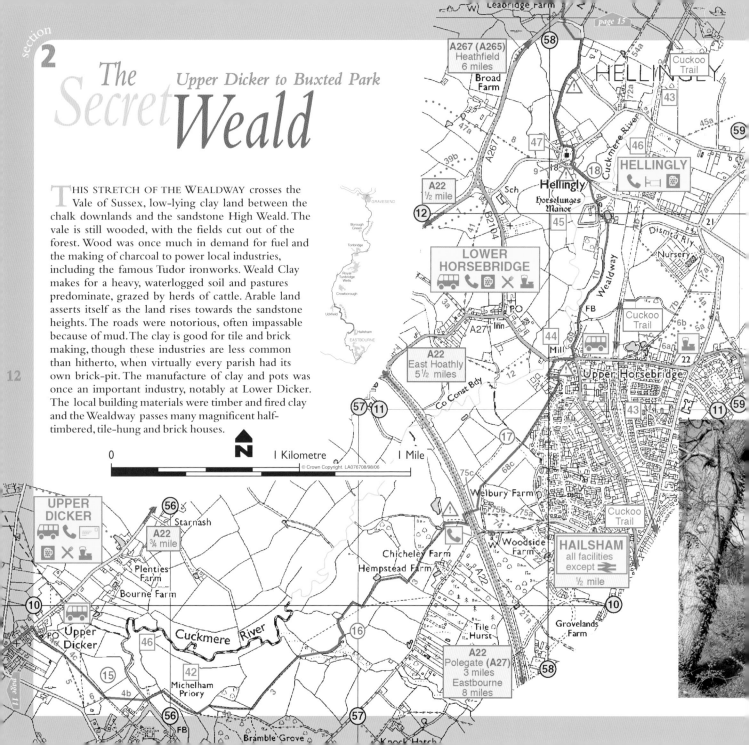

0   1 Kilometre   1 Mile

© Crown Copyright. LA076708/98/06

HELLINGLY

A267 (A265) Heathfield 6 miles

Broad Farm

Cuckoo Trail

A22 ½ mile

Hellingly

Horselunges Manor

Sch

HELLINGLY

LOWER HORSEBRIDGE

Cuckoo Trail

Inn

P.O

A22 East Hoathly 5½ miles

Mill

Upper Horsebridge

Co Const Bdy

Welbury Farm

UPPER DICKER

Starnash

Plenties Farm

Bourne Farm

Chicheley Farm

Hempstead Farm

Woodside Farm

HAILSHAM all facilities except ½ mile

Upper Dicker

Cuckmere River

Michelham Priory

Cuckoo Trail

Tile Hurst

Grovelands Farm

A22 Polegate (A27) 3 miles Eastbourne 8 miles

Bramble Grove

Knock Hatch

GRAVESEND

Borough Green

Tonbridge

Royal Tunbridge Wells

Crowborough

Uckfield

Hailsham

EASTBOURNE

Leadbridge Farm

Dismtd Rly

Nursery

Wealdway

Map 2a *Upper Dicker* (TQ 553099) — *Leabridge Farm* (TQ 581129)
3¾ miles (6 km), allow 2 hours Grade 1 B/C

Interesting features

LOWER DICKER (TQ 565113)
Lower Dicker was once the centre of a local pottery industry, the Dicker and Boship potteries, situated next door to each other on the main road. The Dicker closed in the 1950s but the Sussex pottery industry is commemorated by the name of the public house.

COLDHARBOUR LANE (TQ 560105)
The lane from Upper Dicker to Lower Dicker runs quite straight and its name, Coldharbour, suggests an origin as a possible Roman road.

Michelham Priory

42 MICHELHAM PRIORY
A fine stone-built manor incorporating part of an old priory founded in 1229. The priory with its magnificent gatehouse and moat, is owned by the Sussex Archaeological Society. There is also a working water mill.

PEVENSEY LEVELS (TQ 620098)
A wide area of low lying marsh and wetland, situated to the east of Hailsham. In ancient times, this area was under the sea but today it is a remote area rich in bird and insect life.

43 CUCKOO TRAIL
The Heathfield to Polegate railway line was known affectionately as the 'Cuckoo line'. After it closed in the 1960s, it was converted into a 12-mile long (19.2km) footpath and bridleway, now known as the 'Cuckoo Trail'.

44 HORSEBRIDGE MILL
Horsebridge is the site of a old crossing point of the Cuckmere River. There was once a water-powered flour mill and although milling no longer takes place the buildings and entrance are still much in use.

45 HORSELUNGES MANOR
The manor house dates originally from the 15th century. It was restored in the 1920s and is in private hands.

Hellingly village

46 CUCKMERE RIVER
The Cuckmere River rises near Heathfield and meanders across the Weald before cutting through the downs to the sea. It is pronounced 'Cookmere' and probably means 'Cuca's Lake or Haven' though who Cuca may have been, save that he was a Saxon, is lost in the mists of time.

47 CHURCH OF ST PETER & ST PAUL, HELLINGLY
The church dates from Norman times. The churchyard is ringed by trees and raised above the village. It is an ancient burial ground, a 'cric' dating from at least Saxon times.

13

Hailsham

Hailsham is an old-fashioned town with a long history. Mentioned in Domesday, it was granted its market charter in the 13th century. The curfew was rung daily until the 1950s. It has a modern shopping centre and a market.

HERITAGE CENTRE
(TQ 590095)
A museum which has various interesting displays and also relics of the local farming scene and industries.

CHURCH OF ST MARY
(TQ 592095)
The church has its origins in the 13th century. Its flint and stone tower houses the bells which used to toll the evening curfew.

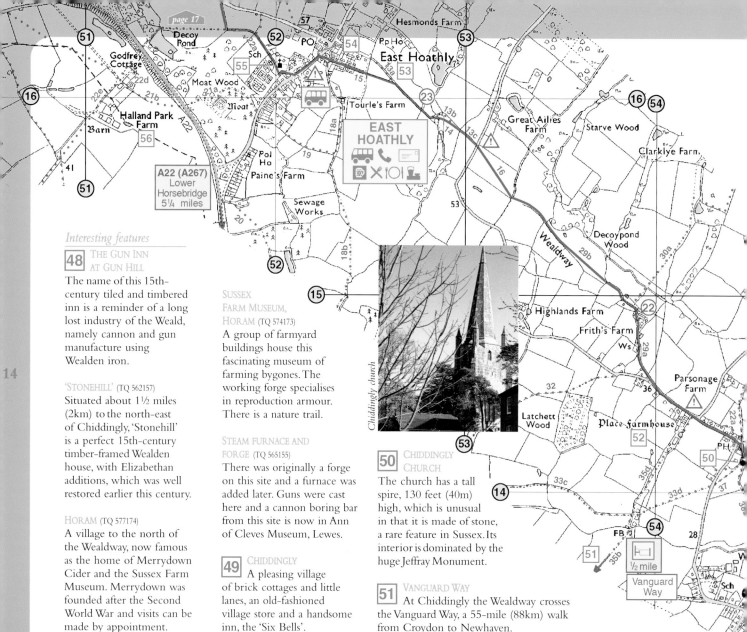

page 17

Map labels (top)

51 · Decoy Pond · Godfrey Cottage · 52 · 55 · PO · 54 · Hesmonds Farm · 53 · PpHo · East Hoathly · Sch · Moat Wood · 53 · 23 · Great Ailies Farm · Starve Wood · 16 · 54 · Clarklye Farm

Halland Park Farm · Barn · 56 · 22d · 22e · 21b · Moat · A22 · 21a · Tourle's Farm · 13b · 14 · 13c · 16 · Decoypond Wood · 30a

41 · 51 · A22 (A267) Lower Horsebridge 5¼ miles · Pol Ho · Paine's Farm · 19 · 18a · 53 · Wealdway · 29b

EAST HOATHLY

20 · Sewage Works · 18b · 52 · 15 · Highlands Farm · 22 · Frith's Farm · Ws · 29a · Parsonage Farm · 32 · 36 · Latchett Wood · Place Farmhouse · 52 · 35d · 22a · P.H. · 50 · 33c · 14 · 33d · 37 · 51 · 35b · FB · 54 · 28 · ½ mile · Vanguard Way · Sch

Chiddingly church

Interesting features

48 THE GUN INN AT GUN HILL

The name of this 15th-century tiled and timbered inn is a reminder of a long lost industry of the Weald, namely cannon and gun manufacture using Wealden iron.

'STONEHILL' (TQ 562157)

Situated about 1½ miles (2km) to the north-east of Chiddingly, 'Stonehill' is a perfect 15th-century timber-framed Wealden house, with Elizabethan additions, which was well restored earlier this century.

HORAM (TQ 577174)

A village to the north of the Wealdway, now famous as the home of Merrydown Cider and the Sussex Farm Museum. Merrydown was founded after the Second World War and visits can be made by appointment.

SUSSEX FARM MUSEUM, HORAM (TQ 574173)

A group of farmyard buildings house this fascinating museum of farming bygones. The working forge specialises in reproduction armour. There is a nature trail.

STEAM FURNACE AND FORGE (TQ 565155)

There was originally a forge on this site and a furnace was added later. Guns were cast here and a cannon boring bar from this site is now in Ann of Cleves Museum, Lewes.

49 CHIDDINGLY

A pleasing village of brick cottages and little lanes, an old-fashioned village store and a handsome inn, the 'Six Bells'.

50 CHIDDINGLY CHURCH

The church has a tall spire, 130 feet (40m) high, which is unusual in that it is made of stone, a rare feature in Sussex. Its interior is dominated by the huge Jeffray Monument.

51 VANGUARD WAY

At Chiddingly the Wealdway crosses the Vanguard Way, a 55-mile (88km) walk from Croydon to Newhaven.

52 PLACE FARM (CHIDDINGLY PLACE)

An imposing brick house with magnificent mullioned

14

Map 2b
Leabridge Farm (TQ 581129) — *East Hoathly* (TQ 519163)
5 miles (8 km), allow 2½ hours Grade 1/3 B/C

windows. It is the only remaining fragment of Chiddingly Place, once the home of the Jeffray family. Sir John was a Baron of the Exchequer in the days of Elizabeth I.

PEKES (TQ 554130)

A privately-owned medieval manor house with an Elizabethan porch. It is reputed to be haunted by

Sir Richard Milward, who is sometimes seen clanking in his armour trying to find his daughter.

53 EAST HOATHLY
East Hoathly is a pleasant village of brick and tile-hung cottages. Once notorious for its right-angled bend on the A22 road, it is now by-passed and wears an air of quiet peace.

54 THOMAS TURNER'S HOUSE, EAST HOATHLY
Formerly the home of the 16th-century diarist and chronicler, Thomas Turner. He told tales of village life in East Hoathly and nearby Halland House.

LAUGHTON PARK (TQ 502149)

Laughton Park, in a remote area of the 'Dicker Waste' to the south, was the former home of the Pelham family before

they moved to Halland House. Only a tower now remains.

55 EAST HOATHLY CHURCH
The church, probably 12th century in origin, was restored and rebuilt in Victorian times but the 15th-century tower was retained. The Tudor doorway is ornamented with the Buckle of the Pelham family.

56 HALLAND PARK
Halland Park Farm is the site of the former home of the Pelham family. Halland House, and some of the outer walls of the house survive. The area is now separated from the village by the by-pass.

15

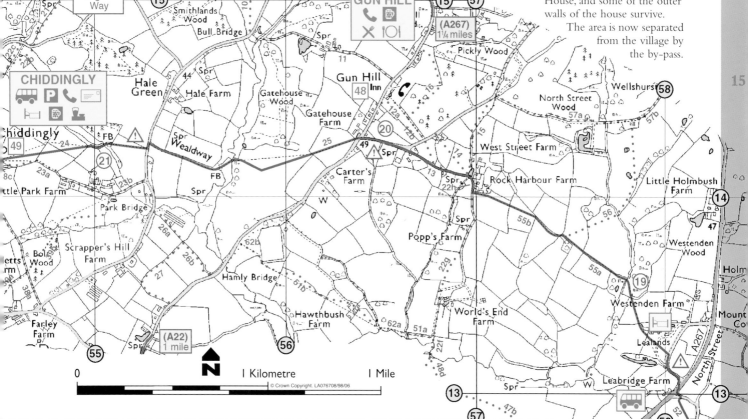

Map 2c

East Hoathly (TQ 519163) –
Newplace Wood (TQ 512197)
3 ½ miles (5.6 km), allow 1¾ hours
Grade 1/3 B/C

Interesting features

TERRIBLE DOWN (TQ 497158)

The down is said to be
named after a particularly
bloody battle. However,
no-one knows to what
battle it refers, perhaps
the Saxon invasion or a
skirmish at the time of
the Battle of Lewes.

57 GREAT WOOD

Its name is now
only a reminder of what
once was here. The area
was felled extensively
and the Great Storm of
October 1987 destroyed
much of the remaining
woodland.

58 SITE OF NEWPLACE
FURNACE AND PONDS

Within the landscaped
grounds is the site of a
former iron-foundry
and the extensive ponds
are the remains of the
hammer ponds.

16

Lake at Old Whyly

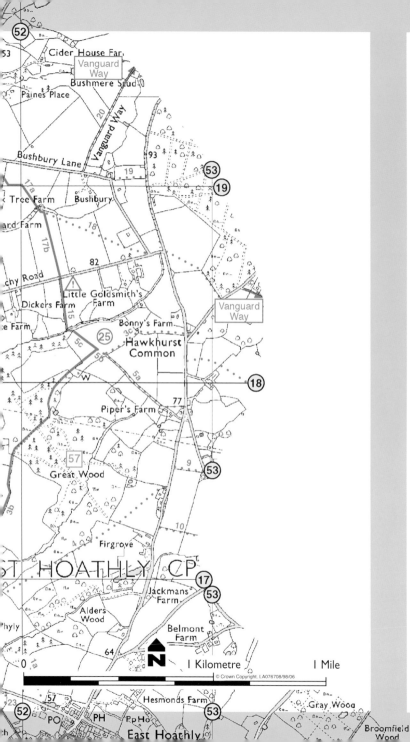

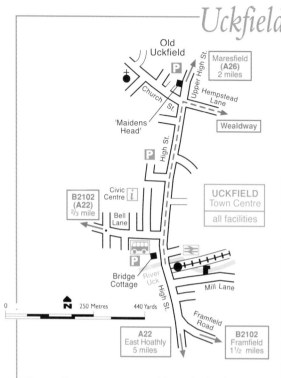

Uckfield

Old Uckfield

Maresfield
(A26)
2 miles

Church St.

Upper High St.

Hempstead Lane

Wealdway

'Maidens Head'

High St.

UCKFIELD
Town Centre
all facilities

B2102
(A22)
2/3 mile

Civic Centre

Bell Lane

Bridge Cottage

River Uck

High St.

Mill Lane

Framfield Road

B2102
Framfield
1 1/2 miles

A22
East Hoathly
5 miles

0   250 Metres   440 Yards

N

17

BRIDGE COTTAGE (TQ 473208)

A superb example of a medieval Wealden hall house, most of the timber structure remaining. It is built on a clay platform, as the land around was marshy. It is now a museum open to the public.

OLD UCKFIELD (TQ 473215)

Old Uckfield is situated at the top of High Street and has many interesting brick, weatherboarded and tile-hung cottages, whilst the more modern town is down by the railway.

'MAIDEN'S HEAD' (TQ 473214)

A large, imposing Georgian inn with bow-fronted windows. At the time of writing it is closed but it should reopen in the future.

LAVENDER LINE (TQ 452171)

The railway now terminates at Uckfield but until 1969 it continued southwards to Lewes. Part of the line, based around Isfield station, is now restored and known as the 'Lavender line'.

18

Map 2d
Newplace Wood
(TQ 512197) —
Buxted Park
church (TQ 486230)

4½ miles (7.2 km),
allow 2¼ hours
Grade 1/2 A/C

Tickerage Mill

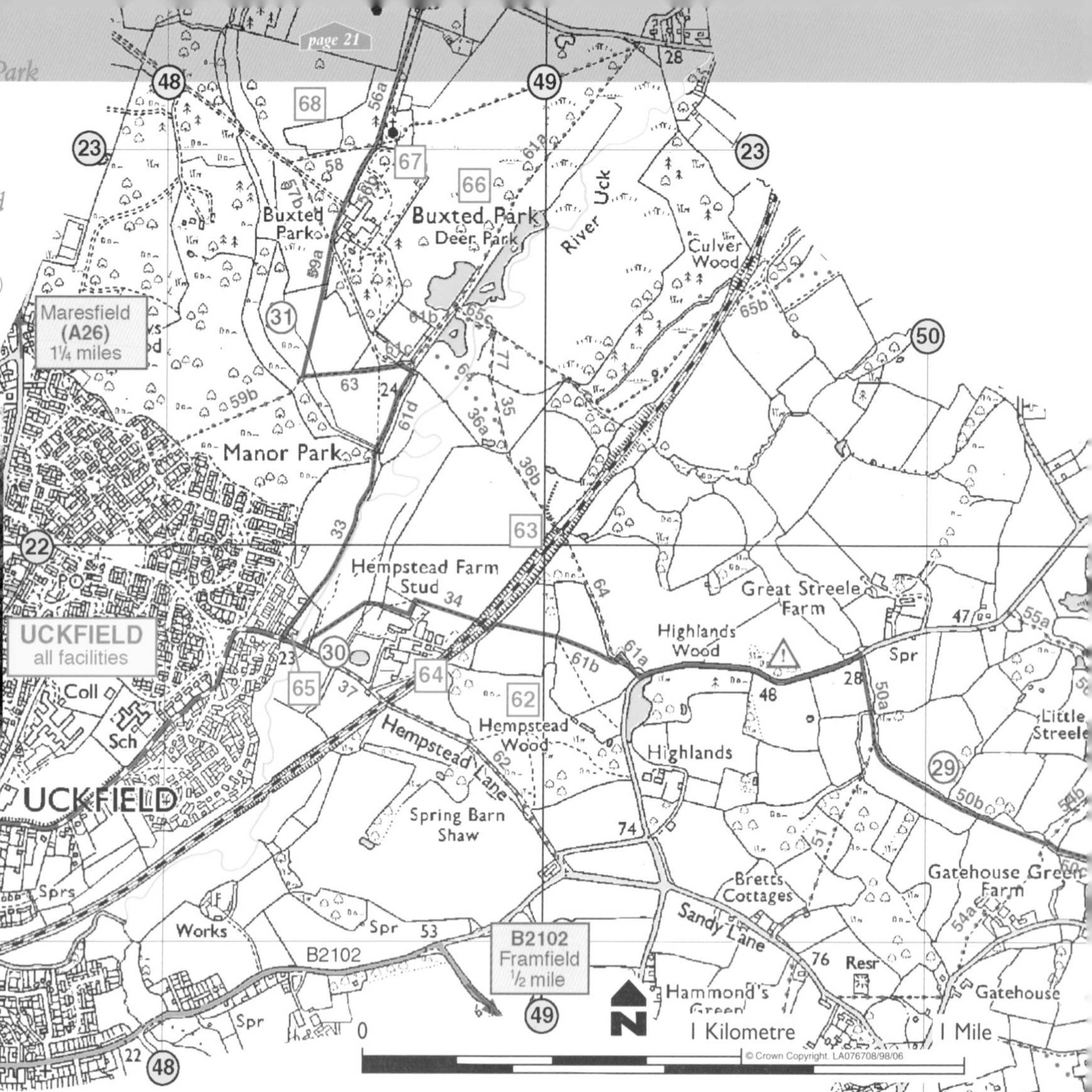

18

page 21

48 68 56a 28
23 58 67 66 49 23
Buxted Park
Buxted Park
Deer Park
River Uck
Culver Wood

Maresfield (A26) 1¼ miles
31 63 24 61d 77 35 36a 65b 50
61b 65c 64 36b

Manor Park 33 36a

22 63
Hempstead Farm Stud 34
Great Streele Farm 47 55a
UCKFIELD all facilities
23 30 64 61b 61a Highlands Wood 48 28 50a Spr
Coll 65 37 62 74 29 50b Little Streele
Sch Hempstead Wood Highlands
UCKFIELD
Hempstead Lane
Spring Barn Shaw 74 51 Bretts Cottages
Sandy Lane 54a Gatehouse Green Farm
PO
(A22) ⅔ mile Sprs F Works Spr 53 B2102 Framfield ½ mile 76 Resr Gatehouse
21 Sta B2102 49 Hammond's Green
East Hoathly 5 miles Spr N
22 48 0   I Kilometre   I Mile
© Crown Copyright. LA076708/98/06

B2102 Framfield ¼ mile 49 Framfield Grange

20 50

Interesting features

17 **WALDRON** (TQ 549193)
A village to the north of the Wealdway which has a notable church with a very wide aisle containing monuments to the Fullers, an ironfounding family. The Star Inn stands opposite the church lychgate, roofed with Horsham slabs.

ST GEORGE'S VINEYARD (TQ 549192)
A leading wine producer in the South East where there are vineyard tours and winetasting. The 11th-century tithe barn houses arts and crafts exhibitions.

59 **BLACKBOYS**
A village of weather-boarded cottages, high in the

Weald. It is well-known for the Blackboys Inn, once a lonely alehouse but later a coaching inn on the turnpike road.

POSSINGWORTH (TQ 535206)
Situated to the north of the Wealdway, Old Possingworth Manor dates from 1657 and has mullioned windows.

Possingworth Manor dates from 1866 and was built for Lois Huth, a man of the city and an art collector.

60 TICKERAGE MILL
The site of Tickerage furnace and forge, where cannon balls have been found. Later it became a corn mill known as the 'Striking Mill'. It was once the home of Richard Wyndham, who wrote

'South-East England' in the famous 1930s Batsford series.

61 MILLS (TQ 505211)
There are two attractive old water mills, both now private houses, situated on the Tickerage stream.

FRAMFIELD (TQ 496204)
A village with some tile-hung and timber-framed cottages. There is also a church, inn and nearby Framfield House.

62 HEMPSTEAD WOOD
The site of iron workings in Roman times, rather than the Tudor Wealden iron industry, emphasising the long tradition of iron working in the Weald.

63 UCKFIELD RAILWAY LINE
The line was opened in 1866 as the East Grinstead, Groombridge and Royal Tunbridge Wells railway. Later a new line was opened from Eridge to Oxted and London and the original line to Royal Tunbridge Wells closed in the 1980s.

64 SUSSEX HORSE RESCUE SANCTUARY
Situated just off the Wealdway at Hempstead Farm, this sanctuary is close to Hempstead Mill.

65 HEMPSTEAD MILL
The former mill at Hempstead, near Uckfield, is now a private house. It is an imposing building with its waterwheel still in place.

66 BUXTED PARK
The present house was built in 1726 but was much altered and added to following a fire in 1940. It is now a country house hotel and conference centre, set in glorious parkland and lakes. Deer roam the park. The famous trees were largely destroyed in the Great Storm of 1987.

67 CHURCH OF ST MARGARET OF SCOTLAND, BUXTED
Standing guard over the site of medieval Buxted village, the origins of the church are 13th century but with later additions and much restored. Wordsworth's brother, Christopher, was rector here for about 50 years and is buried in the churchyard.

68 SITE OF MEDIEVAL VILLAGE OF BUXTED
The original village at Buxted was situated near the church. Lord Liverpool, the owner of Buxted Park, removed the village to its present location in the early 1830s and only the site of the village is now visible in the park.

19

Map 3b

Fairwarp (TQ 474267) —
Car park at Camp Hill (TQ 471300)
3 miles (4.8km), allow 1½ hours Grade 1/4 A/D

Interesting features

73 FAIRWARP
Christ Church was built in 1881 and enlarged considerably in 1930, thanks to the generosity of the Eckstein family. There are monuments to them in the churchyard.

74 OLDLANDS
Oldlands is an ancient site. In 1844, an accidental discovery proved for the first time that the Romans had iron working sites in Sussex. Many Roman coins were also found, covering a period of over 200 years. The iron slag may well have paved the Roman road through the forest.

75 BARNSGATE MANOR VINEYARD
The vineyard is situated at Heron's Ghyll and is a 56-acre (22.66 hec) farm with fine views of the Weald. Tours around the vineyard are available and there is a museum.

76 DUDDLESWELL MANOR
Duddleswell has always been one of the great estates of Ashdown Forest and was once a Royal manor. Today the manor is a 19th-century building but opposite it is the site of the original house.

77 DUDENEY CHAPEL
Near to the Manor are believed to lie the mysterious remains of the Dudeney chapel. In 1855, the surviving parts of an ecclesiastical building were discovered by an amateur archaeologist, the Rev. Edward Turner of Maresfield.

78 DUDDLESWELL COMMON
Duddleswell Common is a large tract of common land on Ashdown Forest centred on Duddleswell which dates from 1693 when 'common' status was legally conferred upon it.

79 TURNPIKE ROAD
A new road was built over the forest in 1766 and there was a tollgate at Duddleswell crossroads. In order to prevent travellers avoiding the tolls, long dykes were built to stop them taking a route over the forest.

80 CAMP HILL
One of the highest parts of Ashdown Forest, Camp Hill commands extensive views over the Weald to the South Downs. The hilltop is characterised by a ring of fir trees.

81 LONDON–LEWES ROMAN ROAD
This road was built to connect London with the iron workings of the Weald and the coast. The road, which crosses Ashdown Forest, can be traced and a small stretch has been exposed and preserved. A descriptive plaque stands a few paces from the Wealdway north-east of Camp Hill.

Map 3c
Car park at Camp Hill (TQ 471300) — *Five Hundred Acre Wood* (TQ 490335)
2¾ miles (4.4km), allow 1½ hours
Grade 1/4 B/D

Interesting features

ASHDOWN FOREST CENTRE (TQ 432323)
Three timber-framed barns house both the administrative centre of the forest and also an information centre which sets out the history of the forest and the wildlife to be found here.

ASHDOWN FOREST FARM (TQ 425315)
Situated at Wych Cross near the Ashdown Forest Centre is a working farm and llama centre. There are also tea and gift shops.

NUTLEY WINDMILL (TQ 451291)
The post mill near Nutley is thought to be the oldest in Sussex. It is a beautiful, entirely wooden, construction and was used to grind corn for the surrounding area. It was restored to full working use in 1981 by the Uckfield and District Preservation Society.

82 KINGS STANDING
Although the name is not that old, this is an ancient site and research has shown large square earthwork enclosures covering about 19 acres (17.69hec). Excavation proves both Roman and prehistoric occupation.

83 ASHDOWN FOREST PANORAMA
For a 360-degree panorama of the Ashdown Forest and the surrounding area, make a short detour to the top of a nearby tumulus. This stands at a height of over 650 feet (200m), one of the highest points of the High Weald.

SITE OF FURNACE & FORGE, NEWBRIDGE (TQ 456326)
The forge was built in 1496 on land belonging to the Duchy of Lancaster. It was the first English blast furnace and appeared to be making cannons by 1509. However, production was very small at only about 160 tons (162.57tn) a year. The last reference to the site is 1603.

84 FIVE HUNDRED ACRE WOOD
This wood was originally planted with beech and oak in the 18th century in a enclosure created in the 1693 decree and owned by Earl de la Warr. The 1987 storm destroyed much of the old timber. It was the original 'Hundred Aker Wood' of A A Milne.

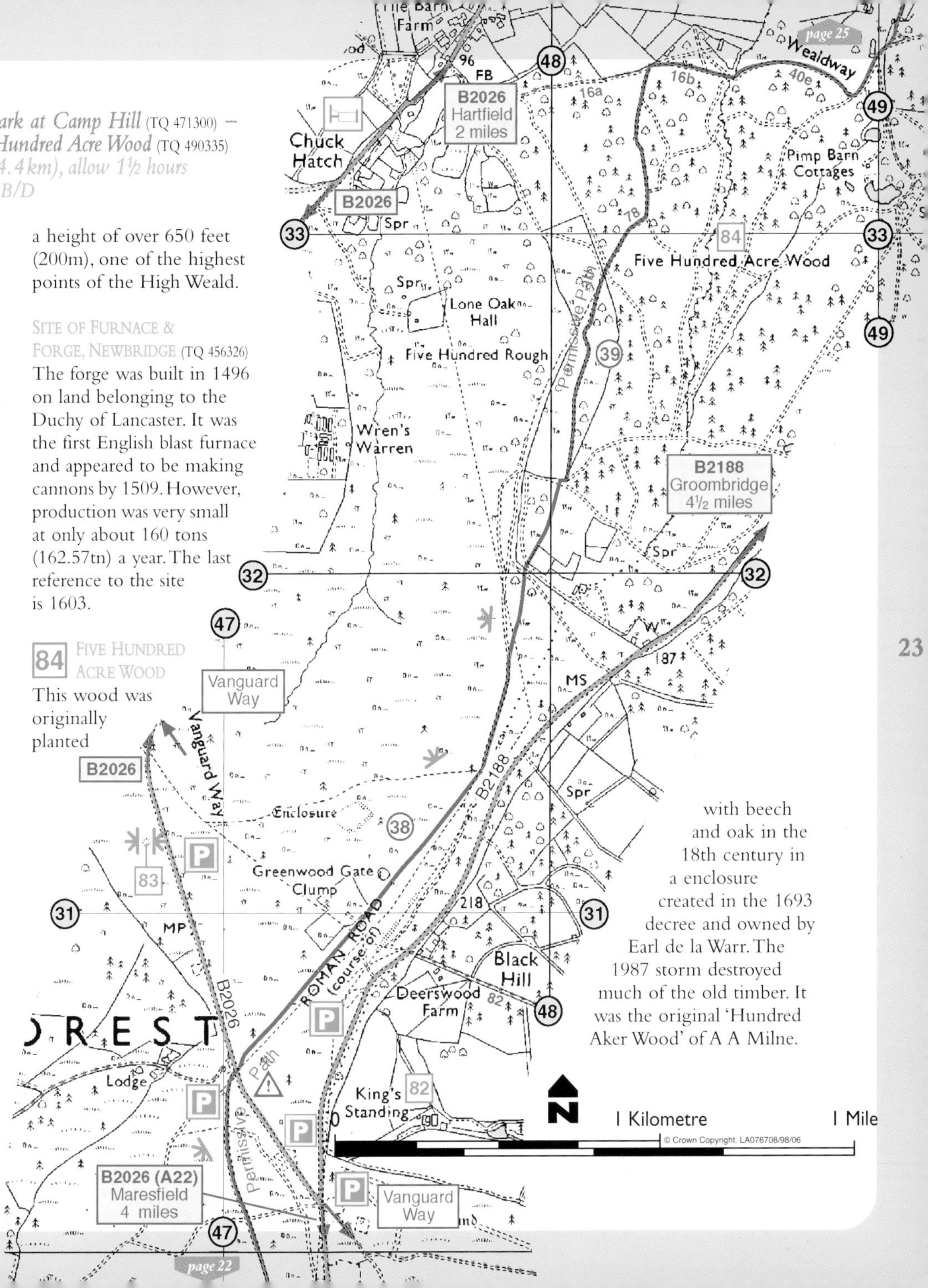

23

© Crown Copyright. LA076708/98/06

1 Kilometre   1 Mile

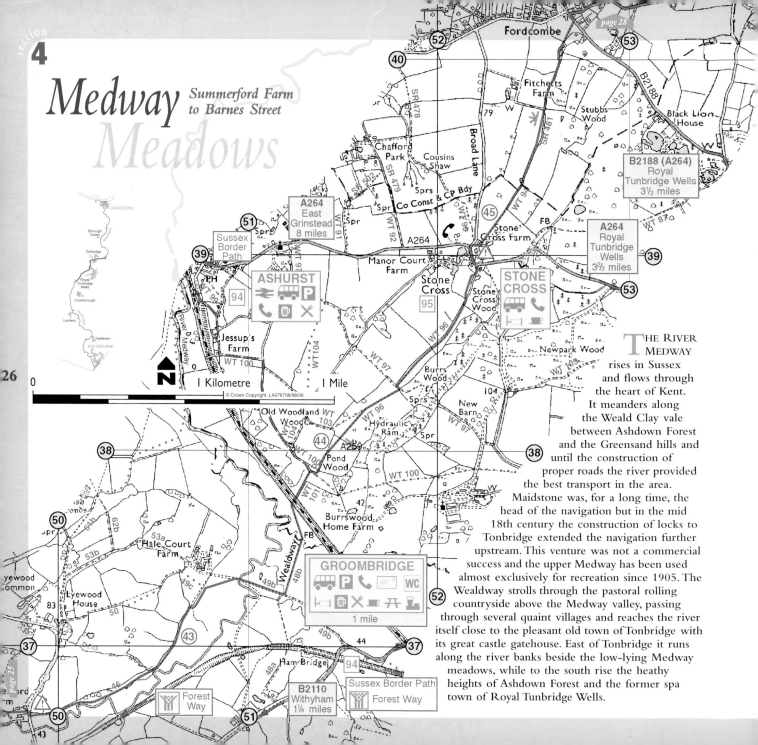

Medway Meadows
Summerford Farm to Barnes Street

GRAVESEND

Borough Green

Tonbridge

Royal Tunbridge Wells

Crowborough

Uckfield

Hailsham

EASTBOURNE

26

Fordcombe

page 28

52

53

B2188

40

Fitchetts Farm

Stubbs Wood

79

W

Black Lion House

SR 478

Broad Lane

YV

Chafford Park

Cousins Shaw

SR 502

SR 479

Sprs

Spr

Co Const & CP Bdy

SR 481

B2188 (A264)
Royal Tunbridge Wells
3½ miles

WT 87

45

Stone Cross Farm

FB

A264
Royal Tunbridge Wells
3⅔ miles

39

51

A264
East Grinstead
8 miles

WT 91

WT 92

A264

WT 95

Spr

53

Sussex Border Path

Manor Court Farm

Stone Cross

Stone Cross Wood

STONE CROSS

39

PH

ASHURST

94

95

WT 96

WT 101

Newpark Wood

WT 101

River Medway

WT 99

Jessup's Farm

WT 100

WT 104

WT 97

Burrs Wood

104

New Barn

WT 97

1 Kilometre

1 Mile

© Crown Copyright. LA076708/98/06

Old Woodland Wood

WT 103

WT 104

Hydraulic Ram

Spr

New Barn

38

44

A259

38

WT 100

Pond Wood

WT 100

42

50

64b

62b

Burrswood Home Farm

WT 101

53a

Hale Court Farm

Wealdway

FB

GROOMBRIDGE

1 mile

53b

49c

48b

52

50

Lyewood House

Lyewood Common

83

50

49b

37

43

Ham Bridge

44

37

94

37

Forest Way

B2110
Withyham
1¼ miles

Sussex Border Path

Forest Way

50

51

43

THE RIVER MEDWAY rises in Sussex and flows through the heart of Kent. It meanders along the Weald Clay vale between Ashdown Forest and the Greensand hills and until the construction of proper roads the river provided the best transport in the area. Maidstone was, for a long time, the head of the navigation but in the mid 18th century the construction of locks to Tonbridge extended the navigation further upstream. This venture was not a commercial success and the upper Medway has been used almost exclusively for recreation since 1905. The Wealdway strolls through the pastoral rolling countryside above the Medway valley, passing through several quaint villages and reaches the river itself close to the pleasant old town of Tonbridge with its great castle gatehouse. East of Tonbridge it runs along the river banks beside the low-lying Medway meadows, while to the south rise the heathy heights of Ashdown Forest and the former spa town of Royal Tunbridge Wells.

Map 4a *Summerford Farm* (TQ 498367) − *Fordcombe* (TQ 527402)
3¼ miles (5.2 km), allow 1¾ hours   Grade 1/4 B/C

Interesting features

94 SUSSEX BORDER PATH
This 152-mile (243 km) long path follows the Sussex border from Emsworth, Hampshire to Rye, East Sussex and crosses the Wealdway between Ashurst and Groombridge.

GROOMBRIDGE (TQ 530377)
Astride the county border of Kent and Sussex, Groombridge is situated on the river Grom. The Kent part of the village is particularly attractive with the 17th-century Crown Inn and tile-hung cottages grouped around a triangular green.

CHURCH OF ST JOHN, GROOMBRIDGE (TQ 533376)
The church was built in red brick in 1625 as Groombridge Place's private chapel. It contains six stained glass windows by Charles Kempe.

GROOMBRIDGE PLACE AND GARDENS (TQ 533376)
The moated brick-built house was built between 1625 and 1674 on the foundations of the medieval house. The series of exquisite walled gardens, which are open to the public, were laid out under the guidance of John Evelyn.

HARRISON'S ROCKS (TQ 532356)
This fine outcrop of Ardingly sandstone has spectacular cliffs above

Between Stone Cross and Withyham valley

steep slopes. They are named after William Harrison, a firearms maker, who opened them to the public. Today they are very popular with climbers.

SITE OF ASHURST FURNACE AND FORGE (TQ 507390)
Ashurst forge and furnace, on the upper River Medway, produced guns for the Navy.

95 STONE CROSS
A little hillside hamlet with a pond at a double bend on the A264 road. This road was in earlier days known as Sandy Lane and was originally a packhorse track.

FERNCHASE MANOR (ASHURST PARK) (TQ 532395)
This impressive house was built in the 1830s on the site of an earlier house. It is now a residential home.

Groombridge Place

27

Royal Tunbridge Wells

29 ROYAL TUNBRIDGE WELLS COMMON (TQ 577388)
Originally a swine-pasture, the common was heavily wooded before the Great Storm of 1987, when many trees were lost. Now conservators are working to restore the acid heathland ecology of earlier years.

THE PANTILES (TQ 581387)
The famous collonaded shopping area, a 17th to 18th-century shopping precinct, which grew around the main chalybeate spring in the mid 17th century.

MUSEUM AND ART GALLERY (TQ 586394)
Displays include local history and archaeology, natural history, dolls and toys and the famous 'Tunbridge ware', a decorative woodware formerly produced in the town and surrounding villages.

BATH HOUSE (TQ 581388)
Built in 1804 around the chalybeate springs to provide warm vapour and shower baths of mineral water. The famous spring is still open and visitors are served the water in the traditional fashion, by a 'dipper'.

CORN EXCHANGE (TQ 581387)
Built as a theatre in 1801-2 for the flamboyant actress, Sarah Baker, it became the Corn Exchange in 1841 and a statue of Ceres, goddess of the harvest, stands above the entrance.

'A DAY AT THE WELLS' (TQ 581387)
Housed in the Corn Exchange, life-like scenes, sounds and smells conjure up life in the famous spa-town in 1740.

CHURCH OF KING CHARLES THE MARTYR (TQ 582388)
Dedicated to Charles I by Royalist visitors, the church was built in 1676 and enlarged in 1690 when its superb plasterwork ceiling was installed by Henry Doogood, Wren's chief plasterer for St Paul's Cathedral.

WEST STATION (TQ 579385)
The station, built in 1866 and closed in the 1980s, is now open as a restaurant. The nearby engine shed is the headquarters of the Spar Valley Railway.

CALVERLEY PARK (TQ 589393)
Virtually a 'new town' just to the north of 'old' Tunbridge Wells, designed by Decimus Burton from 1828 onwards. Villas are set in a semicircle looking down onto the landscaped Calverley Grounds.

30

Map 4c

Bidborough (TQ 567435) – Tonbridge (TQ 591465)
3 3/4 miles (6 km), allow 2 hours
Grade 1/5 A/D

Interesting features

112 HAYSDEN COUNTRY PARK
Two flooded gravel pits, now used for fishing and water sports, are the main features of this 165-acre (66.77hec) country park in the Medway valley to the west of Tonbridge.

Tonbridge

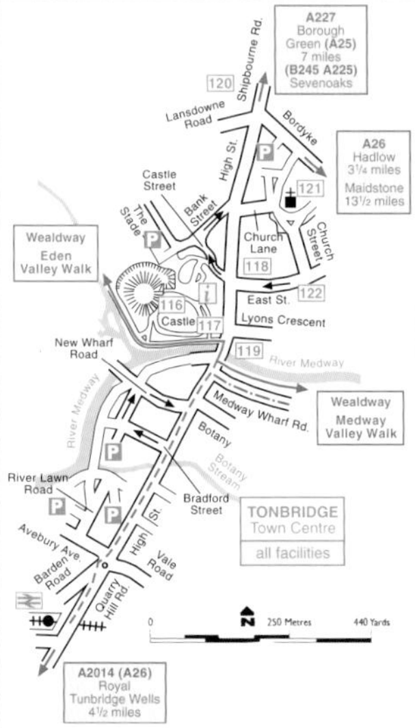

116 TONBRIDGE CASTLE
Originally built by the Normans on the site of Saxon fort, today only the impressive 13th-century gatehouse and part of the curtain walls remain.

117 CHEQUERS INN
This and the adjacent shop are both splendid 15th-century half-timbered houses, with gables and cusped bargeboards.

118 'ROSE AND CROWN'
A famous 16th-century hotel. The chequered-brick frontage dates from the 18th century as does the big porch spanning the pavement.

119 GREAT BRIDGE
The former bridge which was paid for by Henry VIII, replaced an earlier stone bridge of Norman date.

120 TONBRIDGE SCHOOL
The famous public school was founded by Sir Andrew Judd in 1553. Its Victorian buildings have witnessed scenes in the early lives of many eminent writers and cricketers.

121 CHURCH OF ST PETER AND ST PAUL
Dating from the 12th century, the church was restored by Christian in 1877-79.

122 PORT REEVE'S HOUSE
A half-timbered 16th-century house, famed for its oriel windows, where the town's tax collector used to live.

31

113 TONBRIDGE FLOOD RELIEF BARRIER
The barrier which crosses the River Medway near Haysden Country Park was built in 1979–80 to control the river's flow through Tonbridge.

114 POWDER MILLS
Today the site is a chemical works but it was formerly an important gunpowder works.

115 LUCIFER BRIDGE
The name arises from a battle between local people and the landowner in the early 19th century. Someone biblically inclined scrawled "How thou art fallen from heaven, O Lucifer" on the bridge and the name stuck.

57 Powder Mills
114 SR 437A FB
SR 437
MU 24 Wealdway
Works
115 Lucifer Bridge
53
MU 25
Barden Park MU 28
58
59
E V Walk Sch
54 Castle (remains of)
Sports Ground
TONBRIDGE all facilities
TO
page 32

A21 (A225) Sevenoaks 6 miles
FB
Flood SR 435A
Barrier SR 421A
FBs
113 MU 26 SR 42
MU 48
Sharpe's Bridge
Haysden Country Park
MU 29
A2014 (A26) Royal Tunbridge Wells 4½ miles
46
59

46
56 Hayesden Water
Straight Mile
FB
112
MU 46
MU 47
MU 51
52
Lower Haysden
MU 49
MU 50
HAYSDEN
Brook Street Farm
Sch
58

114 POWDER MILLS

MU 60
Manor Farm
Chartwell A21
MU 50
MU 53
A21 (A26 A2014) Tonbridge 1¼ mile Royal Tunbridge Wells 4 miles
45

45

MU53A
CP Bdy
51
A26 (A2014) Tonbridge 1⅓ miles
58

New Plantation
WT 60
WT 61
Beechy Toll
0   1 Kilometre   1 Mile

Birch Wood

-112
51

56 44
Seals Wood
Waghorn's Wood
A26
44
Bidborough Corner
58

B2176 Penshurst 3½ miles
Home Farm
PO
B2126
57
45
A26 Royal Tunbridge Wells 2⅔ miles

56
page 29

Tonbridge castle
G.K.

© Crown Copyright. LA076708/98/06

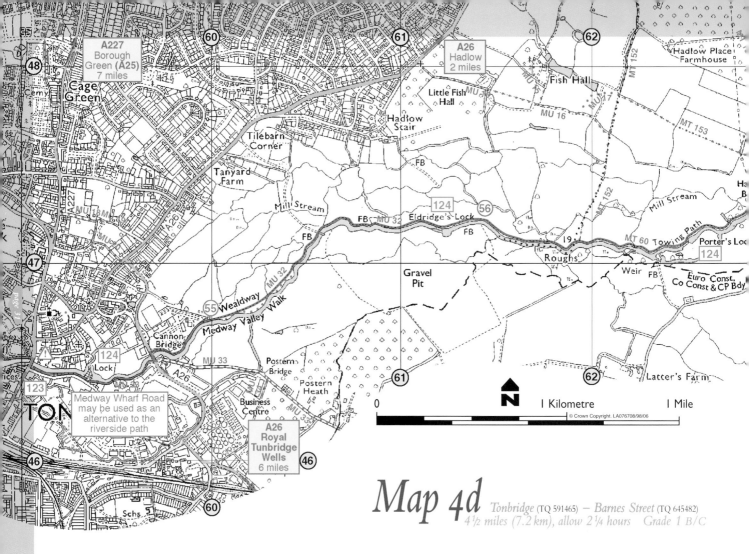

Map 4d
Tonbridge (TQ 591465) — *Barnes Street* (TQ 645482)
4½ miles (7.2 km), allow 2¼ hours   Grade 1 B/C

Interesting features

123 MEDWAY VALLEY WALK
A 28-mile (44.8km) walk along the Medway valley from Tonbridge to Rochester via Maidstone which follows the Wealdway between Tonbridge and just beyond East Lock.

124 MEDWAY LOCKS
The navigation was improved with locks as far upstream as Tonbridge. It was difficult to maintain an even flow of water and the locks are rather small, so trade was never brisk and the river is now used only for recreation. The sluice gates, recently built, are remote-controlled.

125 HARTLAKE BRIDGE
A brick bridge on the site of a Medway tragedy. It was from an earlier timber bridge here that, in 1853, two wagons laden with hop pickers tumbled into the river, drowning 30 of the unfortunate occupants.

126 MEDWAY GRAVEL
The extraction of gravel from the Medway floodplain has increased in recent years

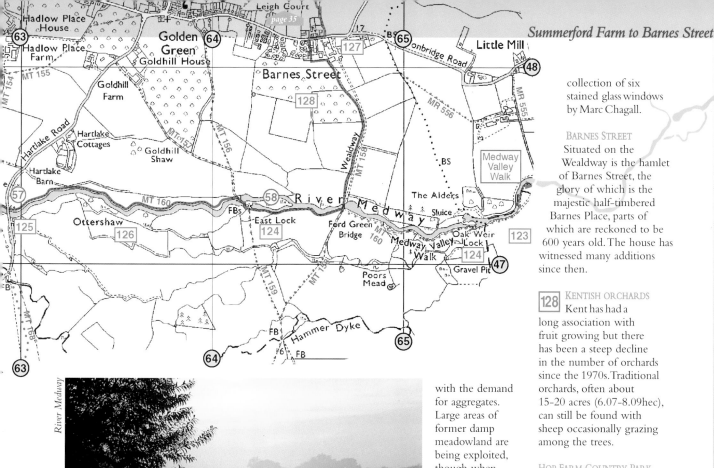

River Medway

collection of six
stained glass windows
by Marc Chagall.

BARNES STREET
Situated on the
Wealdway is the hamlet
of Barnes Street, the
glory of which is the
majestic half-timbered
Barnes Place, parts of
which are reckoned to be
600 years old. The house has
witnessed many additions
since then.

128 ### KENTISH ORCHARDS
Kent has had a
long association with
fruit growing but there
has been a steep decline
in the number of orchards
since the 1970s. Traditional
orchards, often about
15-20 acres (6.07-8.09hec),
can still be found with
sheep occasionally grazing
among the trees.

HOP FARM COUNTRY PARK,
BELTRING (TQ 674475)
Whitbread used to grow
its own hops on its extensive
estate. Today, the hop farm
is a well-known tourist
attraction with the largest
collection of Victorian
oast houses in the world,
32 in all. The Shire Horse
Stables are based here,
together with an
exhibition about the
Kentish hop industry.

with the demand
for aggregates.
Large areas of
former damp
meadowland are
being exploited,
though when
extraction finishes
there will be
compulsory
landscaping with
lakes and
plantings.

127 ### ALL SAINT'S
CHURCH,
TUDELEY (TQ 622454)
South of the
River Medway
across Hartlake
Bridge and hidden
behind a farmyard
is Tudeley church,
remarkable for its

33

The
Garden of
England

Barnes Street to the Pilgrims' Way

WHEN HENRY VIII'S FRUITERER planted his Kentish orchards in 1533 he began the tradition of fruit growing in the county which, together with the production of vegetables and hops, has earned Kent the title 'Garden of England'. This section of the Wealdway saunters among some of Kent's remaining orchards and hop gardens, as well as plantations of 'Kentish cobs', the big hazelnuts beloved of the Victorians. These mid-Kent orchards are planted on the slopes of the Greensand hills, which provide an excellent soil for fruit, and on that part of the Medway lowlands where the Weald Clay is buried by sandier deposits. There are several attractive villages on or near the Wealdway: West Peckham with its village green; Hadlow with its pleasing main street and gothic folly, Hadlow Tower; Plaxtol with its working forge and the 'model' village of Mereworth. To the north the Greensand drops away into the Vale of Homesdale and its curious collection of neolithic long barrows.

Kent House Farm, near Barnes Street

Map 5a
Barnes Street (TQ 645482) – *A26 road* (TQ 652516)
*3¼ miles (5.2 km), allow 1¾ hours
Grade 1 B/C*

Interesting features

HADLOW TOWER
(TQ 634498)
The tower stands 170 feet (51.8m) high and dominates this part of the walk. It is also known as 'May's Folly', after its builder, the eccentric industrialist Walter May, who built it so tall in an attempt to see the sea. He failed and the folly was left to its fate.

HADLOW COLLEGE
(TQ 629498)
Situated just outside the village, the college offers education and training in agriculture, horticulture and related subjects. The impressive Broadview Gardens and garden centre are open to the public.

ST MARY'S CHURCH, HADLOW (TQ 634497)
The church was rebuilt in Victorian times but the tower and spire date from the 14th century. It houses a chair reputed to have belonged to Miles Coverdale but probably a (very good) fake. In the churchyard is a memorial to those who drowned in the Hartlake Bridge disaster.

129 KENT HOUSE FARM
Among the orchards, there is a complex of six converted oast houses opposite the farm.

130 CROWHURST FARM
An impressive collection of converted oast houses visible from the Wealdway.

Barnes Street

PUBLIC FOOTPATH

page 37

65
62
MR 368
Grove House
MR 522

A26 Mereworth 1½ miles

66

A228 (A26) Mereworth 1⅓ miles

MR 517
46
Mount Pleasant Farm

A26 Hadlow 1⅓ miles
MR 516
MR 518

Goose Green
51
MR 517
51
MR 519
MR 520
KM 89
¼ mile
MR 521
65
Resr

A228 East Peckham 2 miles

Peckham Place Farm
Hextall Court

anford Lane
Pond Farm
MR 519
61

MR 526
65
Crowhurst Farm
MR 523
130
MR 624
Crowhurst Hop Farm
MR 525

50
MR 527
24
FB
50
MR 53
Wealdway
Peckham Bush

PECKHAM BUSH
MB 532
MR 533

HADLOW all facilities except 🚂 ¾ mile

MR 523
MR 533
Bullen Lane
MR 533
W
MR 523A

28
MT 147
MT 150
129
Kent House Farm
60
MR 560
Hatches Lane
Style Place Farm
49
49
MT 148
Style Place House
MR 560

64
MT 149
BS 18
Pierce Mill Lane

EAST PECKHAM all facilities except 🚂 ½ mile

GOLDEN GREEN
MT 136
MT 136
FB
Pierce Mill
River Bourne
MT 151
MT 150
59
BSs
Addlestead

N

1 Kilometre   1 Mile
0
66
© Crown Copyright. LA076708/98/06

64
65
onbridge Road
Ppg Sta

LITTLE MILL
Little Mill

House
page 33

35

Hadlow Tower

Map 5b
A26 road (TQ 652516) — *Shipbourne Forest* (TQ 626546)
3½ miles (5.6 km), allow 1¾ hours   Grade 2/3 A/D

Interesting features

ST MICHAEL'S CHURCH, EAST PECKHAM (TQ 662522)
High on a hilltop (360 feet, 110m) above the Medway valley, this redundant church commands superb views. It was originally Norman but has much 14th and 15th-century work.

ROYDON HALL (TQ 666517)
The hall, built in 1535, was heavily restored in about 1870. Its gardens include spectacular 15th-century terraces. The property is now a centre for the international transcendental meditation movement.

131 WEST PECKHAM VILLAGE GREEN
A charming corner of the Garden of England, where the village green nestles under the shadow of the Norman church tower. The peaceful green is surrounded by trees, barns and former oasthouses; a classic Kentish scene.

132 DUKE'S PLACE, WEST PECKHAM
The 15th-century Duke's Place was once a manor of the Knights Hospitallers. It is large, half timbered and L-shaped. After a fire in 1500, part was rebuilt with traceried windows but there are still ancient beams and screens.

133 GREENSAND WAY
A 108-mile (172.8km) long-distance path from Haslemere in Surrey to Hamstreet in Kent, following the line of the Greensand hills. It crosses the Wealdway at West Peckham.

YOTES COURT, WEST PECKHAM (TQ 651534)
Yotes Court, situated to the north-east of the village, is a red-brick house of 1658, perfectly and pleasingly built. It makes for a wonderful setting, particularly in spring, when admired across the waving swathes of daffodils. It is now a hotel.

134 CHURCH OF ST DUNSTAN, WEST PECKHAM
The church has a Norman tower and an early 14th-century aisle and chapel. There is a handsome screen, a Norman font, a 17th-century pulpit and various tombs. The most remarkable feature is a raised chapel, fitted with a family pew for the local squire, surrounded by oak columns and tombs.

135 OXEN HOATH
The current house dates from the late 18th or early 19th centuries and is built of ragstone.

136 GOVER HILL
To the west of the Wealdway, Gover Hill stands at 450 feet (138.5m) on the edge of Mereworth Woods. The hill is a National Trust viewpoint, with excellent views southwards over the Weald towards Tonbridge.

MEREWORTH (TQ 660538)
Mereworth is pronounced 'Merry-worth'. It was built in the 1740s by the Earl of Westmoreland to replace the old village demolished to make way for Mereworth Castle.

137 MEREWORTH WOODS
One of the biggest stretches of ancient forest surviving in Kent which includes Shipbourne Forest. It is now mostly coppiced with areas of grassy heathland.

ST LAWRENCE CHURCH, MEREWORTH (TQ 660538)
Built in 1746 of Kentish ragstone, this is regarded as the best 18th-century church in Kent. The spire of the church is quite a local landmark and is in fact a copy of the spire of St. Martin-in-the-Fields in London.

View from Gover Hill

36

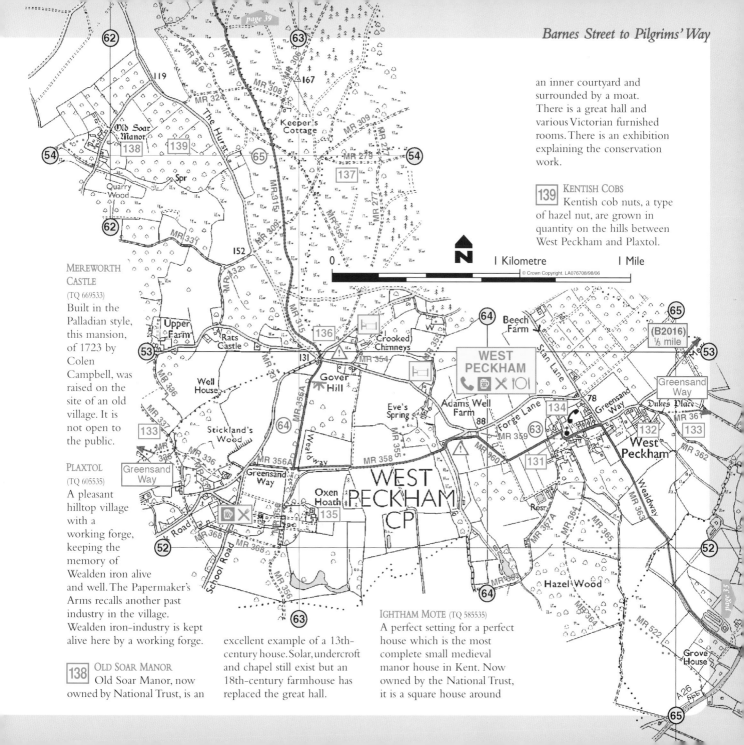

an inner courtyard and surrounded by a moat. There is a great hall and various Victorian furnished rooms. There is an exhibition explaining the conservation work.

139 KENTISH COBS
Kentish cob nuts, a type of hazel nut, are grown in quantity on the hills between West Peckham and Plaxtol.

MEREWORTH
CASTLE
(TQ 669533)
Built in the Palladian style, this mansion, of 1723 by Colen Campbell, was raised on the site of an old village. It is not open to the public.

PLAXTOL
(TQ 605535)
A pleasant hilltop village with a working forge, keeping the memory of Wealden iron alive and well. The Papermaker's Arms recalls another past industry in the village. Wealden iron-industry is kept alive here by a working forge.

138 OLD SOAR MANOR
Old Soar Manor, now owned by National Trust, is an excellent example of a 13th-century house. Solar, undercroft and chapel still exist but an 18th-century farmhouse has replaced the great hall.

IGHTHAM MOTE (TQ 585535)
A perfect setting for a perfect house which is the most complete small medieval manor house in Kent. Now owned by the National Trust, it is a square house around

Map 5c *Shipbourne Forest* (TQ 626546) – *Wrotham Heath* (TQ 634580)
2½ miles (4 km), allow 1¼ hours   Grade 1/3 A/C

Interesting features

140 GREAT COMP GARDEN
The brick-built house dates from about 1600 and may have once been larger. There are mullioned and transomed windows. The garden extends for several acres and comprises a wide variety of trees, shrubs, heathers and herbaceous plants. It is open to the public daily in the summer.

141 PLATT
This pleasant hamlet merges to the west with new developments spreading from Borough Green. Nearby 'The Hopfield', which was designed by Colin Lucas, a leading modernist architect of the 1930s, as his weekend cottage, is a classic statement of the modern movement.

142 CHURCH OF ST MARY, PLATT
The Church of St Mary was built in 1841-42. A cruciform church with a good solid tower built in the 15th-century, and an enormous hammerbeam roof, with a welter of flying arches. Only the thinness of the timbers show it to be a fake, albeit a good one, and by no means the only one in the Garden of England.

143 POTTERS HOLE, PLATT
The Wealdway passes close to a pit which must have connections to the former Wrotham pottery, a 17th-century pottery with a distinctive style known as 'Wrotham Ware'. It is perhaps the first English pottery for which we have information on the potters and artists. Examples are in Maidstone Museum and the British Museum.

144 WROTHAM HEATH
The 761-feet high (232m) Wrotham Hill has one of the finest views near this stretch of the Wealdway, looking north to the Thames estuary.

145 SWANLEY TO MAIDSTONE RAILWAY LINE
The line opened in the 1860s as a single track branch. It was doubled by 1875 and electrified in the 1930s. It is a useful relief line to the main railway between London, Ashford and Dover but is quite heavily graded, which made the line hard work for steam engines.

38

'The Blue Anchor', Platt

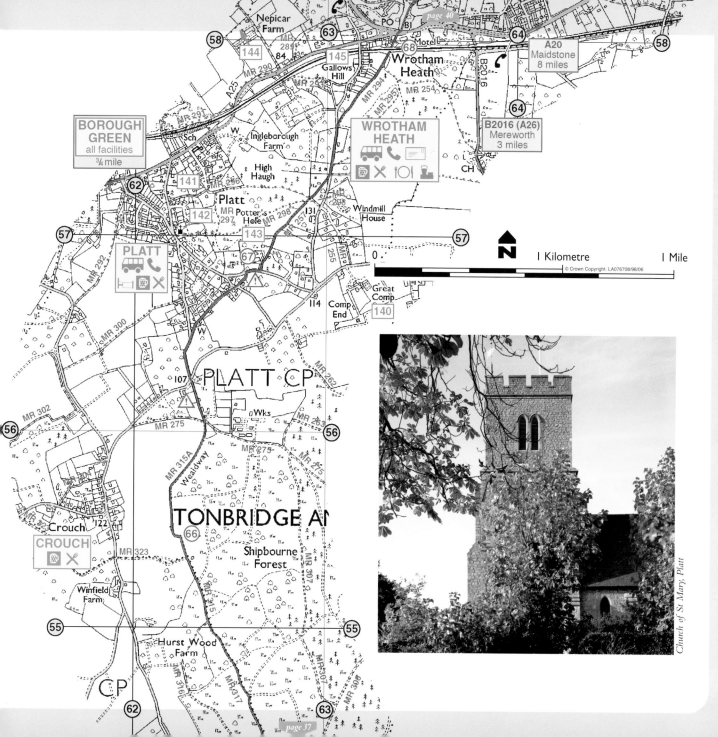

Nepicar Farm

MR 289

84

page 40

58

144

63

PO BI

68 Motel

Wrotham Heath

64

A20
Maidstone
8 miles

58

145

Gallows Hill

MR 290

A25

MR 291

Sch

MR 294

MR 254

MR 295D

B2016

64

B2016 (A26)
Mereworth
3 miles

CH

BOROUGH
GREEN
all facilities
¾ mile

W

Ingleborough Farm

High Haugh

CH

WROTHAM
HEATH

🚌 📞 ✉️
🛏️ ✕ 🍴 ⛽

62

141

MR 296

Platt

MR
297

MR Potter's
Hole

142

131

Windmill House

57

143

MR 298

57

0

N

1 Kilometre   1 Mile

© Crown Copyright. LA076708/98/06

PLATT

🚌 📞
🛏️ 📷 ✕

67

255

MR

⚠️

114

Great
Comp

Comp
End

140

MR 292

MR 300

W

39

107

PLATT CP

⚠️

Wks

MR 302

MR 262

56

MR 275

56

MR 315A

MR 275

MR 263

MR 315

Crouch

122

TONBRIDGE A

66

Shipbourne
Forest

MR 307

CROUCH

📷 ✕

MR 323

MR 316

MR 315

MR 307

Winfield
Farm

55

55

62

Hurst Wood
Farm

MR 317

MR 307

MR 308

63

CP

Church of St Mary, Platt

Map 5d

Wrotham Heath
(TQ 634580) —
Pilgrims' Way
(TQ 653613)
*3 miles (4.8 km),
allow 1½ hours
Grade 1/3 A/C*

Looking from the North Downs

40

North Downs Way

Pilgrims' Way

65

66

61

71

MR 197A

MR 182

61

156

FE CP

Sprs

Long Barrow

P

MR 182

MR 146

154

MR 187

MR 184

155

81

MR 183

Wealdway

Ryarsh Wood

TROTTISCLIFFE

½ mile

60

MR 183

60

149

MR 165

½ mile

Leneys
Cottages

70

Woodgate

MR 164

56

MR 165

68

Woodgate Road

MR 184

Little
Woodgate

Sand Pit

MR 165

MR 167

MR 161

64

Resr

M20 (A20)
Maidstone
7 miles

148

M20

152

MR 170

59

59

Burial Chamber
(rems of)

Long Barrow
(rems of)

153

Pit
(dis)

MR 172A

MR 175

MR 168

151

59

M20
Swanley

Westfields
Farm

150

148

ADDINGTON

66

147

69

St
Vincents
Waterfalls

Addington Park

M26 (A20)
Wrotham
Heath
1 mile

Jord
Place

ADDINGTON
CP

CH

A20
Maidstone
7 miles

146

Wealdway

MR 173

63

Shaw
Hill

MR 175

MR 175

A20

64

Hotel

PO

81

58

65

58

65

Wrotham
Heath

B2016 (A26)
Mereworth
3 miles

Mount
Offham

Test

0   1 Kilometre   1 Mile

N

page 43

page 39

Interesting features

146 NEPICAR FARM
A working farm with milking sheep and rare breeds of various types, including pigs and goats. There is also cheesemaking and lots of home-grown produce.

147 FORD PLACE, WROTHAM HEATH
An interesting place, which appears to be the remains of a Elizabethan or Jacobean mansion. It is a two-storeyed brick house, with mullioned windows built to look as thought they are made of stone rather than brick. Inside are remnants of an earlier house, together with a fine stone chimney in an upper room. The house is now virtually on the hard shoulder of the M26 motorway.

148 M20 AND M26 MOTORWAYS
The Wealdway crosses the M20 motorway just before its junction with the M26. The M20 is the Swanley to Folkestone motorway, whilst the M26 connects the M20 to the M25, running for the whole of its short length at the base of the North Downs escarpment.

149 VALE OF HOMESDALE
The name given to the clay vale between the steep southerly facing scarp of the North Downs and the Greensand ridge. It is thought to have acquired its name from the large quantity of Holm Oak trees which grew in profusion here on the clay soil.

150 ADDINGTON
Known in the Domesday book as 'Eddingtune', this village has some lovely old houses set around a green. The Angel Inn dates from the 14th century.

151 CHURCH OF ST MARGARET, ADDINGTON
Situated on the top of a little hill, the 15th-century tower looms high above the building. Inside, the church contains some Norman walling, though the structure seen today is basically 13th century.

152 THE CHESTNUTS, MEGALITHIC TOMB
A small, partially restored, chambered barrow excavated in 1957 to reveal nine cremations and a couple of infant burials. The burials were dated on the evidence of Windmill Hill and late neolithic pottery. Evidence exists to show that the site was also occupied in mesolithic and again in Romano-British times.

153 CHAMBERED TOMB
A second neolithic tomb is found in Addington Park, a 198 feet long and 36 feet wide (61 x 11m) chambered tomb which was cut in two by

Trottiscliffe church and cottages

the construction of the park road to the now-demolished Addington Place. The barrow is in need of restoration but it is easy to see the eight upended stones which are the remains of the burial chamber at the north-east end of the barrow.

TROTTISCLIFFE (TQ 641602)
Pronounced 'Trosley', this attractive village is tucked away down narrow lanes.

154 CHURCH OF ST PETER AND ST PAUL, TROTTISCLIFFE
The church, set apart from Trottiscliffe down a lane, is dominated by the big pulpit from Westminster Abbey.

155 FORMER PALACE OF BISHOPS OF ROCHESTER
Near the church of St Peter and St Paul is a cluster of

several buildings, including walls that once surrounded a palace of the Bishops of Rochester.

TROSLEY COUNTRY PARK (TQ 633611)
Trosley Country Park covers 160 acres (64.75hec) of the North Downs and is crossed by three waymarked paths, one leading to the Coldrum Stones. There is a visitor centre. The site is owned and managed by Kent County Council

156 COLDRUM STONES LONG BARROW
This neolithic long barrow was excavated in 1910 and given to the National Trust in 1926. It resembles the barrows of north-west Europe, rather than other British long barrows, and contained the remains of 22 people.

41

Downland
and
Estuary
Pilgrims' Way to Gravesend

T HE NORTH DOWNS, the chalk hills that run along the northern rim of the Weald, present their steep scarp face to the south. This steep slope is mostly wooded and traversed by a number of east - west trackways of undoubted antiquity. The best known is the Pilgrims' Way. Above, on the undulating crest of the downs, is much woodland. The Wealdway saunters over the downs, passing along the 'Bowling Alley', a magnificent dip-slope combe near the quaint hamlet of Luddesdown. The combe was saved from threatened Ministry of Defence use in 1982 by the intervention of conservation groups. The downs drop gently northwards to the Thames estuary, crossed by the famous Watling Street, Rome's first British road and now the busy A2 road. The northern terminus of the Wealdway is the historically fascinating seafaring town of Gravesend. The Wealdway passes by many interesting buildings, including ancient Luddesdown Court and Nurstead Court, the magnificent Elizabethan Cobham Hall, Cobham College, the Yeoman's House and Milton Chantry at Gravesend.

GRAVESEND
Borough Green
Tonbridge
Royal Tunbridge Wells
Crowborough
Uckfield
Hailsham
EASTBOURNE

Map 6a

Pilgrims' Way (TQ 653613) — *Bowling Alley* (TQ 671647)
2³⁄4 miles (4.4 km), allow 1 ½ hours
Grade 1/5 B/C

Boughton Street Farm

Interesting features

157 NORTH DOWNS
The North Downs is a great chalk escarpment that separates the Thames valley from the Weald with its steep scarp face to the south. This steep south slope is wooded along much of its length, for this range of hills is capped in many places by residual deposits of clay-with-flints allowing trees to flourish on the otherwise thin chalk soils.

158 PILGRIMS' WAY
This prehistoric trackway runs along the North Downs. It has been used throughout history; after Thomas Becket's martyrdom in 1171, it became associated with pilgrims on their way to his shrine at Canterbury and was named the 'Pilgrims' Way' in Victorian times.

159 NORTH DOWNS WAY
The North Downs Way is a 142-mile (227.2km) long-distance footpath from Farnham to Dover. For most of its length, the path keeps to the North Downs and for part of the way follows the Pilgrims' Way.

160 HOLLY HILL
The Holly Hill viewpoint commands views southwards over the Vale of Homesdale to the Greensand hills.

161 DODE DESERTED VILLAGE
On this remote site near Great Buckland there was once a little village. The village succumbed to the Black Death in 1348 and as a result became deserted.

North Downs Wa

Ｐ WC

¾ mile

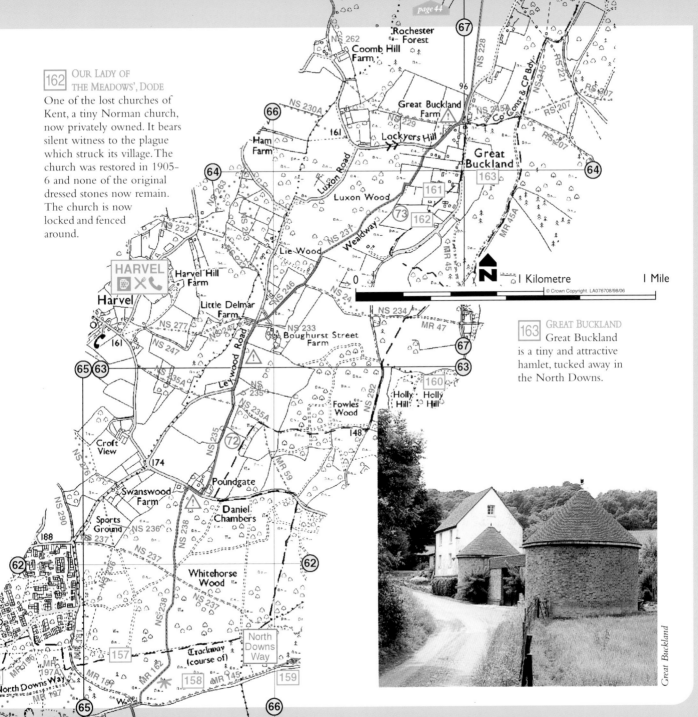

162 OUR LADY OF THE MEADOWS', DODE

One of the lost churches of Kent, a tiny Norman church, now privately owned. It bears silent witness to the plague which struck its village. The church was restored in 1905–6 and none of the original dressed stones now remain. The church is now locked and fenced around.

163 GREAT BUCKLAND

Great Buckland is a tiny and attractive hamlet, tucked away in the North Downs.

43

Great Buckland

page 44
page 40

© Crown Copyright. LA076708/98/06

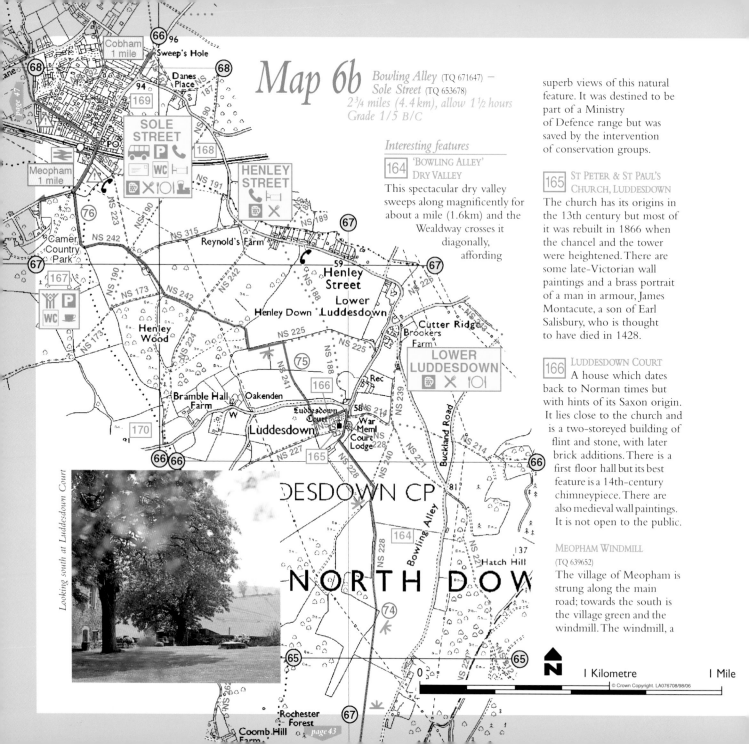

Map 6b

Bowling Alley (TQ 671647) —
Sole Street (TQ 653678)
2¾ miles (4.4 km), allow 1½ hours
Grade 1/5 B/C

Interesting features

164 'BOWLING ALLEY' DRY VALLEY

This spectacular dry valley sweeps along magnificently for about a mile (1.6km) and the Wealdway crosses it diagonally, affording superb views of this natural feature. It was destined to be part of a Ministry of Defence range but was saved by the intervention of conservation groups.

165 ST PETER & ST PAUL'S CHURCH, LUDDESDOWN

The church has its origins in the 13th century but most of it was rebuilt in 1866 when the chancel and the tower were heightened. There are some late-Victorian wall paintings and a brass portrait of a man in armour, James Montacute, a son of Earl Salisbury, who is thought to have died in 1428.

166 LUDDESDOWN COURT

A house which dates back to Norman times but with hints of its Saxon origin. It lies close to the church and is a two-storeyed building of flint and stone, with later brick additions. There is a first floor hall but its best feature is a 14th-century chimneypiece. There are also medieval wall paintings. It is not open to the public.

MEOPHAM WINDMILL
(TQ 639652)

The village of Meopham is strung along the main road; towards the south is the village green and the windmill. The windmill, a

Looking south at Luddesdown Court

Map labels: Cobham 1 mile, Sweep's Hole, Danes Place, SOLE STREET, HENLEY STREET, Meopham 1 mile, Camer Country Park, Reynold's Farm, Henley Street, Lower Henley Down, Luddesdown, Henley Wood, Cutter Ridge, Brookers Farm, LOWER LUDDESDOWN, Bramble Hall Farm, Oakenden, Rec, Luddesdown Court, War Meml, Court Lodge, Luddesdown, Buckland Road, DESDOWN CP, Hatch Hill, NORTH DOW, Rochester Forest, Coomb Hill Farm

page 47, page 43

1 Kilometre   1 Mile

smock mill built in 1801, was said to be a demonstration mill and therefore well-built. It is built on a hexagonal base and the upper part is built of black weatherboarding with white sails and a boat-shaped cap.

167 CAMER COUNTRY PARK
Situated on the B2009 road just to the north-east of Meopham village, Camer Park extends to 46 acres (18.61hec). It is a pleasant, mature parkland with a small area of woodland.

168 RAILWAY
The railway between London and Rochester along the North Downs was opened in stages, this part being built in 1860. It is a line of heavy gradients with saw-toothed profiles and

sharp curves which used to test steam locomotives to the limit. Sole Street station is the highest point on the line at the top of the Sole Street Bank, five miles (8km) at 1 in 100 from Rochester and sea-level.

169 YEOMAN'S HOUSE, SOLE STREET
A half-timbered Wealden house, with a high hall. It was restored by Sir Herbert Baker, the architect who lived at Owlets. It is now owned by the National Trust and is open by appointment.

170 LONDON COUNTRYWAY
A 206-mile (329.6km) round-London route which follows the Wealdway between Sole Street and Gravesend.

Cobham

THE LEATHER BOTTLE INN
(TQ 670685)
This is an ancient inn, frequented by Charles Dickens and featured in his classic work, 'Pickwick Papers'. His patronage has meant that the place of the 'Leather Bottle' on the tourist trail is assured. Even so, the inn wears its fame lightly. It is little changed in décor and atmosphere since the days when Dickens used to stop by for refreshment.

CHURCH OF ST MARY MAGDALENE (TQ 669684)
Famous for its unique set of monumental brasses, the largest in the world, which range in date from 1320 to 1529.

COBHAM COLLEGE (TQ 669683)
Originally a chantry college, these beautiful buildings have been almshouses since the Reformation and still house retired people.

OWLETTS (TQ 665688)
A fine red-brick two-storeyed house with a hipped roof, dating from 1683. It

was extended in 1700. Later additions were made by the architect Sir Herbert Baker, who lived here.

COBHAM HALL (TQ 684689)
Cobham Hall is a superbly proportioned Elizabethan brick mansion set in a wonderful parkland. Its glory is the gilt hall with a gilded plaster ceiling finished in 1672. About a hundred years later an organ was installed and it became a music room, with galleries. In the south wing there is also a fine staircase. Now a girls' school, it is open to the public at certain times of the year.

45

Map 6c *Sole Street* (TQ 653678) – *Tollgate (A2 road)* (TQ 643712)
3 miles (4.8 km), allow 1½ hours   Grade 1/2 A/C

Nash Street

46

Interesting features

171 ST MILDRED'S CHURCH
A flint and ragstone church of the 15th century with many memorials to the Edmeades family.

172 NURSTEAD COURT
A small medieval house of which only part remains following the building of a new house in 1837. The Edmeades family have lived here for over 400 years and the house is open by appointment.

173 IFIELD COURT
A late 18th-century house of brown brick, which is rather tall and austere. Attached to the house are the remains of a medieval building which preceded the current structure, a rectangular flint building with a 15th-century upper window.

174 CHURCH OF ST MARGARET, IFIELD
A small roughcast church with a white weatherboarded western spirelet. The windows on the south side survive from older days.

175 WATLING STREET ROMAN ROAD
The old A2 road between Rochester and London is named Watling Street, the most important Roman road in Britain, linking the channel ports with London. Although the road is now much built over, its origin is shown by the straight alignment.

Nurstead Court

Ifield church

A227
Gravesend
2 miles

TOLLGATE

Motel

65

71 64

71

NU 28

A2

175

BS

A2
Medway
Towns

Wrotham Road

79

NU 9

Watling Street

NU 29

Channel Tunnel Rail Link
(under construction)

NU 18

67

Church Road

NU 32

174

NU 29

70 70

Huntondown
Wood

Ifield
Court

173

NS 176

New
Cottages

NU 41

From 1999, for about four
years, the Wealdway will
be affected by the
construction work for the
Channel Tunnel Rail Link
just south-east of Tollgate.
Take special care, read
the notices and follow the
temporary diversion signs.

47

A227

NU 31

170

Church Road

78

NU 31A

Nash Street

72

Nash Bank

NU 33

69 69

49

NU 36

Cozendon
Wood

Tollingtrough
Green

BS BS

BS

NS 248

NS 282

BSs

NU 34

NU 185

Wrotham Road

Park Hill

NS 248

Nurstead
Wood

Nurstead
Court

172

The
Park

Mill Hill

NS 282

Copt Hall Road

84

NS 185

COBHAM

P WC

¾ mile

NS 185

NS 185

Round
Street

66

NS 185

96

Sweep's Hole

NS 187

77

NS 304

NS 186

0 1 Kilometre 1 Mile

171

© Crown Copyright. LA076708/98/06

N

68

Gdns

A227
Borough Green **(A25)**
7⅔ miles

64

Lordscroft
Shaw

White Post Lane

Sole
Street

65

94

Danes
Place

66

68

NS 190

Gold
Street

Meopham

page 48

page 44

Map 6d

Tollgate (A2 road) (TQ 643712) —
Gravesend (TQ 653744)
2 ½ miles (4 km), allow 1 ¼ hours   Grade 1 A

Interesting features

176 WINDMILL HILL
    Just south from the centre
of Gravesend is Windmill Hill
from which a magnificent
view may be had of the
Thames, still a busy working
waterway, over to Essex and
out to the estuary and the sea.

THAMES ANS MEDWAY
CANAL (TQ 656743)
The former canal between
the Thames at Gravesend
and the Medway at Strood
has been closed for many
years. Today, the basin at
Gravesend is used as a marina.

SHORNMEAD FORT (TQ 692748)
A fort built by General
Gordon in 1860s and
twinned with Coalhouse Fort
on the Essex bank, to guard
the Thames estuary.

TILBURY FORT (TQ 651753)
Alongside the river is Tilbury
Fort, which has a gatehouse
dating back to 1682. There
are the remains of a rampart
and ditch of an older camp
where Queen Elizabeth I may
have reviewed her troops at the
time of the Spanish Armada.

TILBURY DOCKS (TQ 634755)
Now that the London docks
are no more, Tilbury is the
pre-eminent
port on the
London river.
Once it was
one of the
great passenger
ports with a
floating
landing
stage over
1,100 feet
(308m)
long
which
could
be used
by the

48

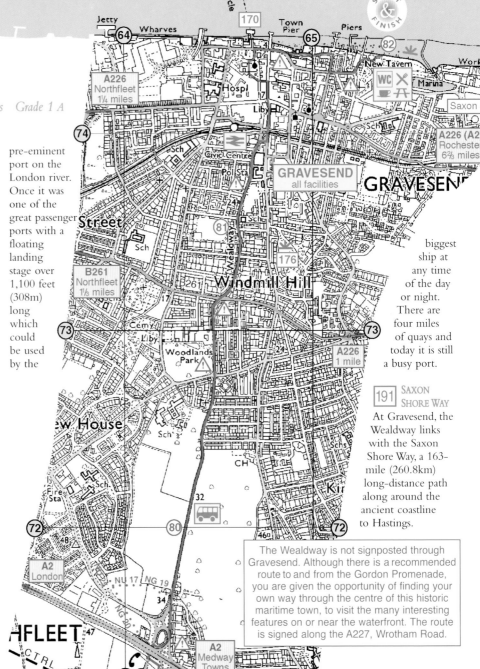

biggest
ship at
any time
of the day
or night.
There are
four miles
of quays and
today it is still
a busy port.

191 SAXON
SHORE WAY
At Gravesend, the
Wealdway links
with the Saxon
Shore Way, a 163-
mile (260.8km)
long-distance path
along around the
ancient coastline
to Hastings.

The Wealdway is not signposted through
Gravesend. Although there is a recommended
route to and from the Gordon Promenade,
you are given the opportunity of finding your
own way through the centre of this historic
maritime town, to visit the many interesting
features on or near the waterfront. The route
is signed along the A227, Wrotham Road.

Gravesend

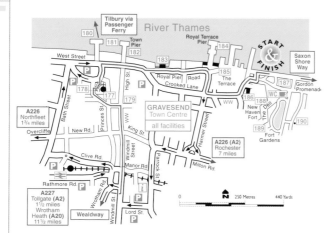

177 ST GEORGE'S CHURCH
Following an earlier fire, the church was rebuilt in 1731-33 with money used from a coal tax raised to help pay for 50 new churches around London. It is a brown-brick building with a big west tower and later additions. It has a 1764 organ.

178 STATUE OF POCAHONTAS, ST GEORGE'S CHURCHYARD
St George's is the last resting place of Pocahontas, the daughter of Powhattan, the over-king of the Red Indian tribes. She married John Rolfe and came to England, where she died in 1617. The statue in the churchyard, by W O Partridge, erected in 1952, is a replica of one in Jamestown, Virginia. The church has two windows placed in her memory.

179 GRAVESHAM MUSEUM
Situated in the High Street is a museum with excellent local material, including many Roman remains found at Singlewell, south of Gravesend.

180 FERRY
There has been a ferry between Gravesend and Tilbury since early times and recorded as long ago as 1304. A vehicle ferry ceased in 1964 following the building of the Dartford Tunnel. The passenger ferry continues to operate.

181 RIVER BOATS
The ferry tradition at Gravesend continues today with pleasure cruises up to the Thames Barrier and Westminster and for the more adventurous, down to Southend-on-Sea.

182 TOWN PIER
Now no longer used and rather decayed but due for restoration, the Town Pier retains its classical Greek Doric columns. It was built in 1842-43 by the engineer J B Redman.

183 ST ANDREW'S ARTS CENTRE
Situated right on the Thames, St Andrews was originally built in 1870 as a mission chapel for seamen. It still has its original stained glass windows commemorating those who died aboard Franklin's ships, HMS Erebus and HMS Terror, in the Arctic in the 1840s. It is now an Arts centre.

184 ROYAL TERRACE PIER
Pilot boats set out from here to guide ships to and from the London river.

185 ALEXANDRA HOUSE
Headquarters of the Port of London Authority's Thames Navigation Service outside which stands the Poseidon sculpture by Sean Rice.

186 CHANTRY HERITAGE CENTRE
Situated near the Customs House, this is an 18th-century brick building incorporating Gravesend's oldest building, Milton Chantry, refounded in 1322 as Milton Hospital. It has flint walls and a 14th-century roof. It is now a museum.

187 GORDON PROMENADE
Overlooking the River Thames, this promenade is named after General Gordon who supervised the construction of the Thames forts, in 1865-71, before taking up the governorship of the Sudan where he was killed attempting to defend Khartoum in 1885.

188 NEW TAVERN FORT
Originally built as a defence against Napoleon in 1780, the earthwork battery is constructed above fascinating underground magazines of Victorian age.

189 FORT GARDENS
These are pleasant grounds adjacent to New Tavern Fort. General Gordon lived at Fort House, destroyed by enemy action during the Second World War.

190 STATUE OF GENERAL GORDON
An excellent statue of General Gordon by John Broad stands in Fort Gardens. It dates from the 1890s and shows Gordon leaning against a tree trunk.

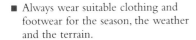 # A Walker's code

- Always wear suitable clothing and footwear for the season, the weather and the terrain.

- Allow plenty of time to complete your walk; normally reckon on walking 2 or 2½ miles (3.2 or 4km) an hour.

- Most public paths cross private estates and farmland; enjoy the countryside, but please have regard for its life and work.

- Avoid interfering with or disturbing things which are connected with a farmer's livelihood.

- Always keep to the paths to avoid trespass and remember that you only have a right of passage on a right of way. Walk in single file through a crop.

- Keep dogs under close control at all times and preferably on a lead across farmland.

- Take special care when crossing or walking along country roads; keep to the side which gives greatest safety, in single file and keep a good lookout for traffic.

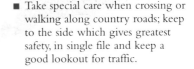

The Wealdway was created and developed by the Sussex and Kent Areas of the Ramblers' Association.
The route is maintained by East Sussex and Kent County Councils.

16 How do you gain information about where to walk in the countryside?

Local paper ☐

Tourist information centre ☐

Word-of-mouth ☐

Local radio ☐

District/county council ☐

Library ☐

Country park/ visitor centre ☐

Local radio ☐

Bookshop ☐

Poster/leaflets (where from) ☐

....

Other (write in)

....

17 Are there any other comments you would like to make about either the route or the guidebook?

....
....
....
....
....
....
....

18 Would you consider purchasing Ordnance Survey maps for walking in the countryside?

Yes ☐

No ☐

19 Have you, or do you intend to purchase the Landranger and/ or Explorer maps associated with this guidebook?

Yes ☐

No ☐

Report form

If you found the Wealdway difficult to follow, what improvements would you like us to make?

....
....
....
....

Please report to us any problems which you came across on any of the paths which form part of the Wealdway, by quoting the page number and one of the following numbers:

Page number [_____]

Ordnance Survey grid reference (e.g. AB 123456) [_____]

Path number (e.g. AB 123) [_____]

Problem ....
....
....
....
....
....
....

It would be particularly helpful if you could photocopy the page and mark the location with a cross or an arrow.

Officers in the Rights of Way Units of East Sussex and Kent County Councils will try to rectify the problem as soon as possible.

Thank you

Thank you for your help, in return for which we will send you a voucher offering you a 10% discount against selected items from the Kent County Council's wide range of countryside and coast products.

Name: *Mr/Mrs/Ms*.......................................

Address: ....

....

....

....

.... Postcode: ....

Tick this box if you would like to receive more information about Ordnance Survey products ☐

Tick this box if you *do not* wish to receive information about walks in East Sussex and Kent. ☐

Fold 3

BUSINESS REPLY SERVICE
Licence No MA 629

2

Marketing and Publicity Officer
Environmental Management Unit
Strategic Planning Directorate
Kent County Council
Invicta House
County Hall
MAIDSTONE
Kent ME14 1XX

Fold 4 Tuck in to flap opposite and post

THE MEDWAY VALLEY bisects Kent into its traditional halves, with the 'men of Kent' living to the river's east and the 'Kentish men' to the west. The valley has been occupied since prehistoric times and has been a line of communication since earliest days. There are neolithic long barrows, and evidence of Bronze and Iron Age settlements. The Celtic folk are thought to have known the Medway as the 'sweet river', a name derived from their word 'medu' (sweet). The Romans knew it as the Fluminus Meduvaeias. The Saxons called it the Medwaeg - from which the modern name descends. The Normans built several great castles on its banks, the furthest upstream being at Tonbridge. The massive earthen motte rises 100 feet (31m) above the river, but only the 13th-century gatehouse survives intact. Tonbridge is the head of navigation of the river which was historically Kent's main road.

Groombridge village

'Beechy Toll', Bidborough

37

Tonbridge castle

Medway valley

The River Medway 92 rises
in Sussex as several little
Ashdown Forest streams but it
flows into Kent and through
Kent, becoming the most
Kentish river of all. The
Medway flows into the
Thames estuary and for
many years the Mayor and
Corporation of the City of
London were responsible for
its administration, bracketing
it together with the River
Thames itself.

The River Medway is
frequently described as two
rivers; the upper reaches,
tranquil and rural, and the
lower, all cement works and
industry. Of course, this is
only in part true today with
gravel extraction along the
valley and it is doubtful if it
was ever anything more than
a rule of thumb.

Medway navigation

The Medway was for long
the main road in Kent. Over
time many fisheries and mills
were set up along the river's
course, and by the time of the
Normans many such
establishments existed, but
increasingly they became
obstructions to navigation.
Maidstone was the head of
navigation for centuries,
served by small boats able to
lower their masts to pass under
the bridges at Rochester and
Aylesford, but by the 1580s
navigation was possible as far
upstream as Yalding. The battle
between river users, in
particular the Wealden

ironmasters who wanted it for navigation, and the millers who wished to retain their weirs, broke out fiercely in 1600 and in the 1620s, when there was a battle to try to clear the upper Medway navigation to allow timber (for warships) and ordnance to pass downstream to Chatham to help the fight against France and Spain, a scheme halted by the low bridge at Nettlestead and associated fish weirs. It was not until 1664 that an Act was passed to actually clear the navigation and certain 'undertakers' were empowered to build locks and wharves to load and unload iron, ordnance balls, timber and other materials. A further Act of 1739 extended the navigation upstream to Tonbridge, creating 14 locks. The locks were rather on the small size, and this restricted the development of trade along the river, as did the difficulty of maintaining an even flow of water.

In 1828 plans were drawn up for an extension of the navigation upstream from Tonbridge to Penshurst. James Christie was engaged as engineer and he bought the Town Mills at Tonbridge so as to control water rights. The following year he drained the Town Pen stranding all the barges at the wharves and was ultimately bankrupted by the ensuing legal wrangles.

The Thames and Medway Canal was proposed in 1800 but not completed until 1824.

It ran from Gravesend on the Thames to Frindsbury on the Medway near Rochester, and cut out the long estuary journey by way of the Isle of Sheppey. However, it was not a happy venture and the section of the canal through a tunnel was later converted into a railway.

'Chafford Arms', Fordcombe

House at Fordcombe

– were shipped downstream to the London market, while large quantities of coal from northern England came upstream.

Increasingly the upper river

Indeed, competition from the railways virtually destroyed the upper river trade during the latter part of the Victorian era and Maidstone once again became the main port of the upper reaches. From Maidstone the produce of the Weald – fruit, hops, corn and other agricultural produce as well as ragstone, timber and bricks

became used for recreation rather than commerce and in 1905 the Upper Medway Company ceased to trade. In 1911 the Medway Conservancy Board was set up and made a valiant attempt to resuscitate the trade of the upper reaches, by removing some of the locks and enlarging the others. Trade was still wretched, and the

Conservancy was wound up in 1934. In the 1960s the Kent River Authority removed restrictions on the opening of lock gates above Maidstone and helped open up the river to pleasure craft.

Hand in hand with the development of the navigation of the Medway is the question of flood control. The clay vale through which the Medway runs downstream from Tonbridge is quickly saturated and heavy flooding may occur, as in 1968. The largest on-river flood storage area Britain has been created near Haysden above Tonbridge, where flood water can be held back in a temporary lake.

Fordcombe 96

This village, set around its green, stands on a hill above the River Medway. The Church of St Peter was built in 1874 by the First Lord Hardinge. He was a military leader who served under Wellington in the Crimea and later became Governor-general of India.

Penshurst (TQ 526437)

Penshurst is an attractive little village on a warm slope above the confluence of the rivers Eden and Medway. It is dominated by the solid sandstone tower of the Church of St John the Baptist, which dates from the 12th century. Here the Becket Window commemorates the famous Archbishop of Canterbury, murdered in 1170, who had appointed Penshurst church's first clerk. The tiny little half-timbered square beside the church is known as Leicester Square, named after the same man as is its more famous London namesake.

The earliest extant structure at Penshurst Place (TQ 528440) is probably of 12th or 13th century origin, but the house is famous for its magnificent 14th-century great hall, virtually unaltered since it was built soon after the house passed into the hands of Sir John de Pulteney, a merchant banker, in 1338. The house was given to Sir William Sidney in 1552 and has remained in his family ever since. Penshurst was remodelled as an Elizabethan mansion by Sir William's son, Sir Henry Sidney, and it was here that his son was born, the famous Sir Philip Sidney, one of the most remarkable men of the Elizabethan age.

Bullingstone 98

A charming spot where 15th-century cottages line the little lane. Its name may well derive from Baluinch, its first recorded inhabitant, who lived here in the 13th century. Avery's Wood 97 was originally a swine-pasture. Today it is regarded as an excellent example of ghyll woodland.

Speldhurst

Today this is an attractive village in the wooded hills but it is a venerable place, for its parish records date back to 1239, making it the oldest parish hereabouts. The Church of St Mary the Virgin 99 was built in Gothic Revival style by J Oldrid Scott in 1891 to replace a church of 1797 which itself replaced an older church destroyed by lightning in 1791. It is famed for its stained glass, including no less then ten windows in excellent contrasting colours designed by Burne Jones and executed by Morris & Co in 1873-1905. The two windows in the chancel are by Clayton and Bell and the west window is by Kempe. The churchyard is renowned for its natural history (including its lichens and mosses) as well as for the architectural merit of many of the tombstones. The Rectory is ancient; it was originally a Glebe house and parts of it are possibly 800 years old.

The George and Dragon public house 100, said to have

The Pantiles, Royal Tunbridge Wells

been built in 1212, is traditionally the alehouse patronised by victorious Kentish bowmen returning from the Battle of Agincourt in 1415. In later years it had connections with the smugglers of Kent and Sussex and there are tales told of subterranean passages linking the hostelry to the church. The Manor House, built in sandstone during the Victorian era, is famed as the place where Lord Baden-Powell wrote 'Scouting for Boys' while staying here with relations.

Modest Corner 106

There is a dispute as to how this little place may have derived its name: was it from the immodest behaviour of the visitors to nearby Royal Tunbridge Wells who camped here in the 18th century or is it derived from one John Mode of Tonbridge who is known to have lived here in the early 14th century? The

View from Bidborough ridge

Old Cottage and Woods Cottage are two of the original buildings of the little community living beside the grazing land of Southborough Common 107, while the former Beehive public house was originally two farmhouses. It was converted into a brewery in 1857, into a pub in 1873 and finally into cottages in 1997.

Royal Tunbridge Wells

Close to the Wealdway, this is a popular former spa town with an extensively wooded common and elegant shopping centre based on the 18th-century walkway known as 'The Pantiles'.

Royal Tunbridge Wells Common (TQ 577388) covers 250 acres (101.17hec) and overlooks the town. It consists of breezy open 'roughs' and blocky sandstone such as the Wellington Rocks, an outcrop of Weald sandstone and a favourite playground for children. Two of the original 18th-century wells that gave

the town its name lie close to the A26 road. Henrietta Maria (1609-1669), Queen Consort of Charles I, was the first Royal personage to visit Royal Tunbridge Wells. She camped on the common. The Wells grew to be an important spa town, and its position as such was assured when in 1735 the dandy, Richard 'Beau' Nash (1674-1762), was poached from Bath to become the Master of Ceremonies. The titled, the rich and the famous, and those seeking riches and fame, met, mingled and enjoyed themselves at Royal Tunbridge Wells.

The Pantiles (TQ 581385) is the famous colonnaded shopping area, effectively a 17th to 18th-century shopping precinct. The walkways – upper and lower – are on two levels which grew up around the main chalybeate water spring in the mid 17th century.

The Church of King Charles the Martyr, London Road (TQ 582388), is interesting not just because of its dedication given by Royalist visitors to the Wells aiming to counteract the town's strong Puritan element. It was built in 1676 and no architect is named in the list of contributors and disbursements, so there probably was none. The bricklayer was a Mr Green and the plasterwork ceiling – the church's glory – was executed by Henry Doogood,

the chief plasterer of Wren's St Paul's in 1690 when the church was enlarged. Earlier plasterwork in the church is by John Wetheral. It was restored by Christian in 1882, when a short eastern chancel was tacked on, since the original church was oriented north-south. The woodwork in the chancel was brought from St Antholin, a demolished Wren church in the City. In July and August lunchtime concerts are held.

Bidborough 110

This delightful village, high on the hills above the Medway valley, has plenty of old cottages with pretty gardens. Wyatts, which stands in Rectory Drive, dates from just after 1788. The small sandstone Church of St Lawrence 111, with its shingled spire, stands on the brow of a spur with superb views to east and west. The Norman nave and chancel were rebuilt in the 13th century while the south aisle dates from 1876-77. There is some late glass by Morris & Co, the east window in the south aisle being to a Burne Jones design. In the churchyard is a monument by Westacott, to Mary, Countess of Darnley (died 1803).

Haysden

Haysden is a hamlet on a minor road in the lovely Medway valley just west of Tonbridge. At nearby Haysden Country Park 112,

41

the flooded gravel pit has been put to recreational use. North-west of the hamlet is the Tonbridge Flood Relief Barrier 113. Half a mile long and 18 feet (5.4m) high, this barrier can hold back 1,230,000,000 gallons (559,650,000,000lt) of water, being the largest on-river flood storage area in Britain. It was completed in 1980 after the disastrous town flood of 1968; the River Medway flow can now be controlled through Tonbridge. During the construction the river was realigned, the Wealdway route now following the new bank.

Tonbridge

Tonbridge is pronounced 'Tun-bridge' and used to be thus spelt. It is a pleasant old Medway town of some 34,500 souls, dominated by the 13th-century gatehouse of its demolished castle 116. The 13th-century gatehouse is all that survives intact of the Norman and later castle, besieged by William Rufus in 1088 and dismantled by the Parliamentarians. Part of the moat and curtain wall survive, as does the 100-foot (31m) high earthen motte with traces of masonry on top. The landscaped Castle Gardens surround the castle. Today the site is overlooked by the municipal offices built in 1793.

The town grew along the main road and the flood-prone flats beside the River Medway mean that it has not

The Chequers Inn, Tonbridge

spread from the road. The old part of the town lies to the north of the river – the High Street has many attractive 18th and 19th-century buildings – with the newer residential area to the south. The 15th-century half-timbered Chequers Inn 117 on the High Street has a famous swinging sign said to have been put up in the time of Elizabeth I and until quite recently a hangman's noose hung high above the pavement, while the 16th-century 'Rose and Crown' 118, also on the High Street, has an excellent Georgian front with chequered brickwork. Possibly the most famous old house in Tonbridge is the 16th-century half-timbered Port

Barnes Street, near Hadlow

Reeve's House 122 in East Street, once the home of the town bailiff.

The River Medway became a navigable waterway in 1741 thereby boosting the fortunes of the town which developed further following the coming of the railway in 1841. Cricket ball manufacture is the most famous

Tonbridge industry, while hops and timber were its traditional products. Today a variety of light industries is found to the north of the town and the river is no longer a commercial highway but the scene of boating activities including splashing about in hired rowing boats and more sedately-organised boat trips. There is also a river walk, a pleasant stroll, starting at the Victorian cast-iron bridge over the river.

Tonbridge is well known for its school 120, founded in 1553 by Sir Andrew Judd.

Former pupils include Sir Sidney Smith (1764-1840), the novelist E M Forster and the cricketer Colin Cowdrey. Jane Austen's father, George (died 1805) was a master here for a while. Today the school buildings are mostly Victorian gothic but include an entrance quadrangle incorporating a block of 1790 enlarged in 1826.

The late 19th-century Perpendicular gothic-style school chapel was first dedicated in 1902 but the roof and everything inside were consumed by a disastrous fire in 1988. It was rebuilt under the direction of Donald Buttress, Surveyor to the Fabric at Westminster Abbey and rededicated in 1995. This magnificent building is open during term times and the public are welcome to view or attend services there. Regular recitals on the impressive 67-stop Marcussen organ are also given to the public.

The large town Church of St Peter and St Paul 121 was heavily restored in 1879. Nonetheless three Norman windows survive in the chancel which was the original Norman church. This was rebuilt first in the 13th century and the nave added. Later centuries saw many further additions. The reclining effigies and inscriptions survive of Sir Anthony Denton and his wife, he in alabaster, she in stone ◔

The
Garden of
England
*Barnes Street to
the Pilgrims' Way*

*West Peckham
village green, Kent*

GRAVESEND

Borough Green

Tonbridge

Royal Tunbridge Wells

Crowborough

Uckfield

Hailsham

EASTBOURNE

> *Where shall we be when this fruit is set?*
> *When the orchards ring with the harvest song?*
> *And the fruit whose heart is this blossoming sweet*
> *Is the garnered good of a year that's done...*
> Anon

Ryarsh Wood

KENT IS KNOWN AS THE 'GARDEN OF ENGLAND'; the name is fitting since large tracts of the county are excellent for horticulture and it presents to the world the face of a well-kept garden. For many centuries it has produced fruit, vegetables and hops for London. Pliny tells us that the Romans introduced cherries to Kent. After a lapse of many centuries Henry VIII's fruiterer, Richard Harrys, planted his north Kent orchards around Teynham in 1533. The Wealdway runs through one of the two main areas of fruit growing in Kent, the mid-Kent region, which traditionally took advantage of the River Medway to convey its produce to London. Orchards are found on soils developed on the Hythe Beds of the Lower Greensand around Maidstone, with an extension southwards into the Low Weald near Tonbridge. In this area apples are the main crop, particularly cooking apples including the excellent 'Bramley's Seedling'.

Kent's vanishing orchards and hop gardens

Economic pressures have forced the decline of fruit and hop production in England and the change continues apace. None-the-less the Garden of England can still hold up its head, since nearly half the orchards remaining in the country are found in Kent. Many visitors come each spring to follow the designated 'blossom routes' which run along the lanes between the orchards, to stand amazed at the beauty of the blossom and dazed and delighted by its glorious scent.

East Malling Horticultural Research Centre, close to the Wealdway, has encouraged the planting of dwarf stock trees. This means that although the total area under orchards may have declined, the actual production has increased considerably, while both maintenance of trees and harvesting of the fruit have been made much easier. It also means that there are few

Peckham Place Farm, Goose Green

traditional orchards left but some still exist along the Wealdway between Barnes Street and West Peckham. Such orchards are undersown with grass where flocks of sheep graze and here and there is a strategically placed beehive, its inhabitants busy in the blossom. In spring this stretch of Wealdway is a sea of flowering apple trees, the air fragrant with scent, and the noise of the bees is a steady, heady drone. There is rather a different atmosphere at harvest time, just as pleasing, with the blended colours of fruit and mature leaves in the quiet sadness of autumn.

Hops and oasts

Hop gardens are traditionally found in association with orchards, for both fruit and hops are labour-intensive. Kent's famous hop gardens are also sliding away into history. Yet hops are forever associated with Kent where two of the more important varieties bear names of erstwhile Kentish growers; Mr Fuggle grew hops near Brenchley, while Mr Golding grew his type of hops near East Malling. The hop plant, which gives the distinctive bitter taste to beer, is a relative of cannabis and was introduced into Britain during Tudor times. British hop growers face increasing competition from foreign seedless varieties but the development of hop extract which can be produced from seeded or unseeded hops has to some extent helped turn the tide.

Hops die down each winter to grow again the following spring. Their climbing shoots, known as 'bines', have to be trained up strings to an overhead wirework mesh supported by poles. They grow remarkably fast, perhaps six to eight inches (15-20cm) a day! Most plants in a hop garden are female, producing the cones which contain the lupulin which is used in brewing. The cones are dried in oast houses, the modern variety of which are very industrial looking rectangular blocks. The attractive round oast houses, surmounted by white cowls, were mostly built between 1850 and 1900 when there was a much greater area under hops. The Victorians built their round oast houses in the belief that this shape helped create a better draught. They have now been almost universally converted into quaint dwellings, as at Kent House Farm `129` and Crowhurst Farm `130`. However, some are preserved, and the Hop Farm Country Park at Beltring (TQ 674475) has the largest collection of oast houses in the world. Earlier oast houses – the 18th-century ones – are, like modern oast houses, rectangular in shape.

Today hops are 'picked' by machine; once they have been cut down by hand. Traditionally the hop harvest began on the first of September and during the 18th and early 19th centuries the huge amount of hand labour required for the harvest was provided by gypsies who joined the local families at that time. Then, with the massive decline in the rural population witnessed by the middle years of the 19th century, whole families of London's poor, particularly the people of the East End, would journey to Kent to pick hops and enjoy a kind of working holiday, going 'hopping'. They frequently returned home with a large bramley apple, their 'opping apple'. The hoppers continued to come until the late 1950s but today they are no more than a moonlit dream.

Barnes Street `127`

This little settlement is a scattering of houses strung along a lane amid the orchards, though its 'street' name suggests a Roman road hereabouts. Barnes Place, the handsome timbered house, is reputed to date partly from the 14th century.

West Peckham church

Hadlow (TQ 634498)

Hadlow, just over a mile (1.6km) west of the Wealdway along a lane fringed by orchards, lies in the valley of the Bourne, a Medway tributary. The surrounding land is gently undulating and Hadlow is celebrated for its pinnacled tower (TQ 634498), 170 feet (52.3m) high, a landmark for miles around. This is the only surviving part of the gatehouse to the gothic

47

Kent Farm House, Barnes Street

48

birthplace of William Caxton (1422–91), the 'father of English printing'.

St Mary's Church (TQ 634497) is tucked down a little lane away from the main road. Its low timber tower and spire date from the 14th century and there are crosses on the door carved by crusaders. The rest of the church is a Victorian rebuilding. The church houses a chair reputedly owned by Miles Coverdale, Bishop of Exeter, translator of the Bible into English. In the churchyard is a memorial to those who drowned in the Hartlake Bridge disaster **125**

East Peckham

This is a largish Medway village which moved down into the valley from its former site to the north during the 19th century. Holy Trinity Church, of 1841, is on rising ground in the centre of the village and possesses fine views over the valley. Closer to the Wealdway, two miles (3.2km) north of the present village, is the now-redundant Church of St Michael (TQ 662522). Originally built in Norman times, the church was much enlarged in around 1300. It commands an expansive view over the Medway valley to the High Weald from its hilltop site amid beech trees.

Roydon Hall (TQ 666517) is a brick-built Tudor manor house with a remarkable 16th-century terraced garden,

the highest level enclosed by the original turreted brick walls. The hall has the date 1535 over the doorway and was the seat of the important Kentish family, the Twisdens. It is now a centre for transcendental meditation.

West Peckham

This is a lovely spot, a little backwater at the end of the road, and surely everyone's idea of the archetypal English village. In the centre stand the church, manor farm, cottages and Swan Inn, forming a tight cluster by the village green **131** where, from beneath the cool shady trees, you can watch cricket in the summer heat. The village was mentioned in Domesday and seems to have taken the subsequent years in leisurely fashion. The group of old timber and tile cottages, now a private house called Duke's Place **132**, on the Mereworth road near the church, are probably on the site of a manor of the Knights Hospitallers founded here in 1408 by Sir John Colepepper, a noted judge. Yotes Court (TQ 651534), an hotel to the north-east of the village, is a splendid red-brick house of 1658.

The Church of St Dunstan **134** has a Norman tower incorporating Saxon stones but is otherwise heavily restored. It is known for its interesting raised chapel and squire's pew, known as the 'Geary Pew', after the lords

castle built by for Walter Barton May in 1838-40 by the architect George Ledwell Taylor, engineer and architect to the Navy. The tower was nicknamed 'May's Folly' and was said to have been built to get a glimpse of the sea but failing to do so, was abandoned. The crowning pinnacles were damaged by

the 1987 Great Storm and for safety had to be temporarily removed. Hadlow Court Castle, May's house of the 1830s, has been largely demolished, only the lodges and stable court remaining. The village itself is attractive with a main street with many weatherboarded and tile hung houses, and claims to be the

of the nearby manor of Oxen Hoath 135. It stands over the family vault on a raised platform and is equipped with table and chairs. It was originally built by Sir John Colepepper as a chantry for the soul of Henry IV and became the squire's pew in 1548. The wooden carvings of the apostles which stood behind the altar were stolen in September 1997.

Just west of the village, Wealdway walkers traverse the entrance to Oxen Hoath, an avenue once lined by magnificent mature limes. Within two hours, the Great Storm of 1987 felled the lot;

now to be replanted but sadly it will be many years before walkers again enjoy a majestic experience beneath these princes of the natural world.

Not far away to the west is Gover Hill 136, 450 feet (138.5m) high, on the edge of Mereworth Woods. The hill is a National Trust viewpoint, with expansive views southwards over the Weald and the broad Medway valley towards Tonbridge.

Mereworth Woods

Mereworth (TQ 660538) is pronounced 'Merry-worth', a happy name for a place. The woods 137, including

Platt village

Shipbourne Forest, are in fact a fairly large surviving area of ancient forest, where wild boar was still hunted during the reign of Elizabeth I. Today it is mostly coppice and heath and the open glades give snatches of the fine views westwards to the fertile Medway valley.

Mereworth itself is not on the Wealdway but the spire of its church (TQ 660538) is a landmark for many miles around,. This 'model' village was built on a new site in the 1740s by the Earl of Westmoreland after the demolition of the old hamlet and church to make way for Mereworth Castle (TQ 669533). This grand Palladian villa, still a private home, had been built in 1723 by Colen Campbell for John Fane who became Earl of Westmoreland in 1736. Campbell may have been the architect of the new church, built in 1746 and regarded as the best 18th-century church in Kent. It is built in Kentish ragstone with a semi-circular porchway supported on Doric columns, and is surmounted by an attractive but rather incongruous spire with a clock – in fact a copy of the spire of St-Martin-in-the-Fields in London. It is a superb sight glimpsed from between the hop gardens.

Plaxtol (TQ 605535)

This large hilltop village with a long village street lies about one and a half miles (2.4km) west of the Wealdway. Church

Row is a lovely group of cottages near the church which is itself interesting. It has no known dedication but was built by Archbishop Laud and completed in 1649, the year of Charles I's execution. It was restored in 1894. The inn is called the Papermaker's Arms, recalling a past industry in the village, while remembrance of another Wealden industry is kept alive here with a working forge making wrought iron gates and weathervanes.

To the south-west is Fairlawne, an impressive mansion with fine gardens which was once the home of the first Governor of Massachusetts and leading Parliamentarian, Sir Harry Vane the Younger. He was beheaded at the time of the Restoration, in 1622, but his ghost is said to haunt the Wilderness Walk here on the anniversary of his execution, carrying his head under his arm. In 1722 Fairlawne was the birthplace of the poet Christopher Smart, author of the poem beginning *"For I will consider my cat, Jeffrey…"*

Old Soar Manor 138 lies between the Wealdway and Plaxtol, on a twisting lane amid orchards and plantations of Kentish cobs. Old Soar is a very fine 13th-century house once owned by the Culpepper family. The great hall has been replaced by an 18th-century farmhouse but solar, undercroft and chapel remain.

49

Addington 150

This attractive village, with old houses set around its village green in the lovely wooded country of the Vale of Homesdale 149, is in fact an ancient place, for here are two neolithic barrows quite close to each other. 'The Chestnuts' 152 is the name given to a small partially restored chambered barrow excavated in 1957 to reveal nine cremations and a couple of infant burials. The burials were dated on the evidence of Windmill Hill and late neolithic pottery. Evidence exists to show that the site was also occupied in the mesolithic and again in Romano-British times. The other neolithic tomb is a 198 feet long (60.3m), 36 feet (11m) wide long barrow in Addington Park 153, a chambered tomb which was cut in two by the construction of the park road to the now-demolished Addington Place. The barrow is in need of restoration but it is easy to see the eight upended stones which are the remains of the burial chamber at the north-east end of the barrow.

Addington is mentioned in Domesday as 'Eddingtune' and the 13th-century Church of St Margaret 151 contains some Norman walling, while the south chapel has a wagon roof with a painted ceiling. It is dominated by its big 15th-century tower. The Angel Inn dates from the 14th century.

Trottiscliffe (TQ 641602)

There are plenty of weatherboarded houses in this old village which is pronounced 'Trosley', a spelling used for the nearby Trosley Country Park on the North Downs. The small Norman Church of St Peter and St Paul 154 is found down a lane below the North Downs. Several other buildings cluster nearby, including parts of the former palace the Bishops of Rochester 155. Inside, the church is dominated by a huge pulpit with an ornate sounding board brought here in 1874 from Westminster Abbey!

Trosley Country Park (TQ 633611), once the grounds of Trosley Towers, covers over 160 acres (64.75hec) and is crossed by three waymarked paths, one leading to the Coldrum Stones. There is a visitor centre open periodically.

The Coldrum Stones 156

This ruinous neolithic long barrow, set on the south facing slopes of the North Downs, measures 68 feet by 55 feet (21 by 17m) and is outlined by the fallen sarsen stones which would originally have supported the earthen mound. The barrow was excavated in 1910 and the central burial chamber, 13 feet by four feet nine inches (4 x 1.2m), was shown to be divided into two compartments, making it more like the chambered barrows in north-west Europe than in the rest of Britain. The remains of 22 people were discovered and the skeletons had physical similarities suggesting close kinship. Neolithic flint work and pottery was also recovered. The site was given to the National Trust in 1926 in memory of Benjamin Harrison, antiquary of Kent ✿

North Downs

Downland *and* Estuary

Pilgrims' Way to Gravesend

> ❝ *...All I seek is the heaven above*
> *And the road below me...* ❞
> Stevenson

Luddesdown village

Nash Street

THIS NORTHERNMOST section of the Wealdway runs across rolling chalk downland and is bordered to the north by the River Thames. The tree-clad North Downs 157 slope gently to the London river, the tidal Thames at Gravesend, as it is just beginning to widen noticeably to its broad mud-fringed estuary. Both the great Watling Street, Rome's first road on British soil, and the ancient trackway known as the 'Pilgrims' Way', march along the North Downs, soon to be joined by the Channel Tunnel Rail Link. Add to these three long-distance routes the great highway of the Thames, the comings and goings of ships of many ages and nationalities, of invading armies and of friendly commerce, of pirate or merchant, pilgrim or refugee, and the flavour of this section of the Wealdway is that it seems to run at right-angles to most wayfaring through the ages. The local building materials are flint and timber, as well as local bricks and Kentish ragstone.

Pilgrim's Way 158

This prehistoric trackway, for so it is, predating by many centuries the tramping feet wending to Canterbury to honour St Thomas, is in effect the North Downs Ridgeway running from Canterbury along the scarp slope of the downs to Guildford where it joins the Harrow Way. The trackway is in places a hollow way, a sunken lane worn by constant usage and by the elements, particularly running water. The main track, and there are several parallel tracks here, is cleverly positioned some little way up the hill providing a little sunny and dry routeway. The North Downs Way 159 follows the Pilgrims' Way and

the two coincide where crossed by the Wealdway.

Dode 161

High on the downs, over a mile (1.6km) south of Luddesdown and close to Great Buckland 163, lies the deserted village of Dode, left empty at the Black Death. It is now just a couple of houses and a disused Norman church 162 extensively restored in 1905-6. It is a spot almost calculated to bring inward reflections to us all, where the grasses themselves seem to whisper in the wind of life's briefness and uncertainty.

'Bowling Alley' dry valley 164

The Wealdway crosses obliquely a glorious chalkland

53

dry valley known as the 'Bowling Alley' on account of its shape. This partly wooded, partly farmed, hollow in the downs runs for about a mile (1.6km) in a north-east/south-west direction south of Luddesdown. Its big sweeping shape makes it archetypal downland, at one with the sky.

'Battle of Luddesdown'

That the 'Bowling Alley' is still under farmland and woodland at all is due to the efforts of campaigners during 1982-83 when there was a very real threat that it would be turned into an Army mine-laying range. The Ministry of Defence had purchased land at Luddesdown in 1982 but the intervention of conservation groups forced a ministerial inquiry and planning permission for the mine laying range was refused. The MOD then sold the land back into private ownership and the superb sweep of the valley was left undefiled.

Luddesdown

The little hamlet of Luddesdown is tucked away in the wooded hill country on the crest of the North Downs. The main building is Luddesdown Court 166, an ancient manor house dating from about 1200, although some of the walls are not of Norman but of Saxon age, three feet (0.9m) thick and built of local flint. The house is on two storeys with the typical 13th-century first floor

hall with an early 14th-century chimney piece. There is some 16th-century restoration work. Nearby stands the Church of St Peter and St Paul 165 which was rebuilt in 1866 by R P Pope, though its old tower remains, containing in its fabric even older Roman tiles.

Sole Street

This pleasant village, on the hills behind Gravesend, was given its first impetus to grow when the railway arrived in 1860 168. The derivation of its name is not exactly prepossessing, since 'sole' is a Kentish word for a dirty pond, but Sole Street is capable of shrugging off such slander and its best building, the half timbered Yeoman's House 169, is a truly splendid 16th-century Wealden house restored by the architect Sir Herbert Baker who, in 1931, gave it to the National Trust. It is open by appointment. Whoever the prosperous Yeoman who lived here may have been, his house calls to mind the old rhyme:
" A knight of Cales,
A Gentleman of Wales,
And a Laird of the North Countree;
A Yeoman of Kent
With his yearly Rent
Will buy them out all three".

Cobham

About a mile (1.6km) off the Wealdway lies the pretty village of Cobham with its half-timbered Leather Bottle Inn (TQ 671685), known well by Charles Dickens who described

it in 'Pickwick Papers' as "a clean commodious village ale-house". Today it is full of Dickens memorabilia. Cobham was home for four hundred years to the Cobham family, which died out during the reign of James I, but their memorials form the greater part of the famous and unique series of brasses in the church (TQ 669684), the best and biggest collection of such brasses in England. These are in two groups arranged across the chancel floor, with various other brasses to masters of Cobham College scattered

Bowling Alley

clothes and armour from the 14th to the 16th century. Of particular note are those of Lady Joan de Cobham (1320), in her wimple and gown, the second oldest brass in England to show a woman, and Sir John de Cobham (1407), shown holding a model of his college. There are the fine canopied brasses of Sir Reginald Braybrook (1405) and Sir Nicholas Hawberk (1407), two of Joan, Lady Cobham's (1433), five husbands. Another of her husbands was Sir John Oldcastle, Shakespeare's Falstaff.

The Church of St Mary

about in other parts of the church. The 14 brasses of the Cobhams show clearly the changing aspect of both

Magdalene is itself a memorable 13th to 14th-century building, with an imposing wide chancel, home of the famous brasses, and a late 14th-century tower. South of the church, through an archway, stands an interesting group of buildings about a little square incorporating a 14th-century hall on the south and Elizabethan buildings on the other three sides. This is Cobham College (TQ 669683) which was founded as a chantry college in 1362 by John de Cobham, to say masses for the souls of his ancestors. It came into the hands of the Cobhams at the Dissolution and the family refounded it as an almshouse in 1598 putting up the Elizabethan extensions.

Magnificent Cobham Hall (TQ 684689), now a school, stands to the east of the village. It was formerly the seat of the Earl of Darnley and was built in 1584-1602 for Sir William Brooke, Lord Cobham, in warm-coloured brick to the Elizabethan 'E' plan. The central part was built in 1662-70 possibly by Inigo Jones but more probably by John Webb. The great park surrounding the mansion has been shorn to the north and east but still retains its beauty. It was much loved by Charles Dickens who walked here often and indeed took his last walk in the park. The gardens were laid out originally by Humphrey Repton in 1790.

Nurstead Court 172

Just off the Wealdway stands Nurstead Court, most of which was built in about

1837, but which retains part of the original building, saved when the rest was demolished to make way for the 19th-century house. It has been, for many generations, the home of the Edmeades family. About half of the medieval house remains, dating from about 1320. It is an aisled hall, compared to that at Winchester Castle and is built of timber set on stone outer walls only 11 feet (3.4m) high. The huge hipped roof is borne on three pairs of oak piers. The house once had a free-standing kitchen (like that at Stanton Harcourt in Oxfordshire) and is very compact in plan. The ruinous stone tower on the north-west corner is probably a 14th-century defensive tower like that at Stone Castle, near Dartford. South of Nurstead Court stands St Mildred's Church 171 which belongs entirely to the 15th century and is full of memorials to the Edmeades family. The nave and chancel are flint-built and the west tower is of Kentish ragstone.

Ifield Court 173

The present late 18th-century house stands on an old site and as at Nursted, though not as spectacularly, part of a medieval building – this one in flint and greatly altered in appearance – is attached to it to the south. The little roughcast Church of St Margaret 174 was probably built by pilgrims on their way to Becket's

Luddesdown

shrine along the old Roman road, old even in their day. It now has a jaunty white weatherboarded spirelet.

Channel Tunnel Rail Link

The new high-speed railway line will pass under the Wealdway just to the south of the A2 road (Watling Street).

Watling Street – the great Roman road 175

There was a British trackway along the line of Watling Street, the present A2 road, before ever the Romans came and Julius Caesar probably used it in his abortive attempts to subdue the British natives in 55 and 54BC. A hundred years later in AD43 it was used by Roman troops

under Aulus Plautius in the successful drive towards London from their beachhead on the Kent coast at Richborough, via Canterbury and Rochester where the two-day Battle of the Medway was fought. Shortly afterwards the trackway was 'Romanised' by Roman road engineers; properly surveyed, realigned and straightened and then properly built. It was extended south from Canterbury to Dover which became headquarters of the Roman-British fleet. The Watling Street was a great highway. In later years it was used by pilgrims to Becket's shrine at Canterbury. Even later it became an important coaching route. The world has travelled Watling Street.

Windmill Hill 176

Rising above Gravesend is Windmill Hill, formerly crowned by a windmill and earlier than that by a beacon to warn of enemy ships approaching the Thames estuary. From here are panoramic views over Gravesend and the northern edge of Kent to the big sweeping curve of the Thames and the Essex shore opposite as far as Southend. There is still much to see, although the once-immensely busy waterway is a thing of the past.

Gravesend

Gravesend stands on the south bank of the great river, at the point where the River Thames becomes the Thames estuary. There is seaweed on the wooden piles and the tang of salt water is in the air, there are pilot boats, a customs house and the Port of London Authority's building. Gravesend is no longer a port, but its river front speaks of a long history of seafaring. Interestingly, until the early years of this century, Gravesend was also a river resort with a tradition of sea bathing and with associated pleasure gardens at Rosherville. But the Marine Baths fell into disuse and the big buildings were demolished just before the First World War.

It is not known how long ago Gravesend became

associated with maritime things but by the 14th century Gravesend ferrymen were taking passengers up the Thames to London and across the Thames to Tilbury and Gravesend was a place where the well to do landed en route

'Poseidon', Port of London Authority Building

for London. By Elizabethan times fleets were assembled there and Francis Drake, Martin Frobisher and Richard Grenville all knew Gravesend. In 1588 Elizabeth I reviewed her troops at Tilbury Fort (TQ 651753), on the opposite bank, before the arrival of the Spanish Armada. Tilbury and Gravesend have worked in harness for a long while and are still linked by ferry. In the 1880s, before the Tilbury Docks (TQ 634755) were completed, Gravesend acted as the terminal port for weekly P&O voyages to India and the Far East.

In the 17th century the

diarist, Samuel Pepys, frequented Gravesend in his capacity as Secretary to the Admiralty and increasingly it was associated with troop ships. In the 1860s the Gravesend Garrison was commanded by the famous

General Gordon, Fort Gardens

General Gordon, hero of Khartoum, and he organised the building of the twin forts, Shornmead Fort (TQ 692748) on the Kent shore and Coalhouse Fort on the Essex shore, to guard the entrance to the Thames. There is a statue of Gordon 190 in Fort Gardens 189, near New Tavern Fort 188. This earthwork battery was thrown up against Napoleon in 1780 and given brick emplacements by Gordon. Beneath it are a large Victorian magazine and another of 1904 which are being restored and are open in the summer months. The

adjacent wide Gordon Promenade 187, which overlooks the Thames, is a fine place to watch the river and its pageant of shipping. Pilot boats set out from the Royal Terrace Pier 184, since Alexandra House 185

Statue of Pocahontas, St George's churchyard

is the headquarters of the Port of London Authority's Thames Navigation Service and, by long tradition, Gravesend is the spot where pilots board vessels to guide them up the narrowing river.

Over the centuries Gravesend proved to be the last resting place of many an unfortunate traveller, carried sick or dying from ships moored in the Thames. The most famous person buried at Gravesend is Pocahontas, the native American princess, who died at Gravesend in 1617 while awaiting a return passage to America. She is thought to be buried in

Gravesend

an arts centre, which stands directly above the river and was originally a mission church for seamen. It was built in 1870-71 by Street. It has fine stained glass windows commemorating those who died aboard Franklin's ships, HMS Erebus and HMS Terror in the Arctic in the 1840s. Gravesend's oldest building is Milton Chantry

186, part of a leper hospital of 1322.

Gravesend has embarked on a massive improvement programme to restore its many fine historic buildings and to make the town an attractive environment for citizens and tourists alike. It will take many years to complete but visitors will not fail to enjoy the changes thus far. Time allowed for exploration, even for a few hours, will be amply rewarded

Gravesend possesses some good Victorian buildings and

is a vibrant industrial town, with most of the industry to the west away from the quaint and narrow High Street and the flourishing indoor market. The town's whole character is imbued with the great tidal river on whose banks it stands and the large Indian population is partly descended from those who arrived in Gravesend as ships' crews during Victorian times. Unlike any other place along the Wealdway, Gravesend is a product not of the Weald but of the world, of explorations, wars and skirmishes, migrations of people, sea voyages and the sea

57

St George's churchyard, where there is a statue of her **178**. Interestingly, the town's name does not relate to burials – it probably has a far more pleasant meaning, derived from 'at the end of the grove'.

Gravesend has two noteworthy churches, St George's **177** which was rebuilt in 1731-33 after the disastrous fire of 1727 which destroyed most of Gravesend, and St Andrew's **183**, now

Port of London Authority Building, Gravesend

Chapter 7

Walk
planning
& preparation

Walking advice

THE BEST SEASONS for walking the Wealdway are spring and autumn. In spring there is new growth with the buds of the flowers and trees bursting open, whilst autumn brings the myriad of glorious colours. In summer some days can be very humid with the best views obscured by heat haze. The winter months add a new perspective, particularly if there is snow or frost, but allowances must be made for the shorter days and possible muddy paths.

The weather in the south-east corner of England can be as uncertain as anywhere in Britain but in general there is more sun and warmer temperatures than elsewhere. As the weather can vary from coast to coast, and change even between the Downs and the Weald, it is advisable to check the weather forecast beforehand (see Weathercall, page 65).

Allow sufficient time to complete your chosen walk.

If you have never walked long distances before, start with a low mileage and work up to higher mileages after a few days. Ten to 12 miles a day is average. Reckon on walking 2 or 2½ miles (3.2 or 4km) an hour. For most of the year this will give you an opportunity to linger at a view-point, to explore an interesting place, to stop for refreshments, take photographs or study botany.

The distances and times for each section of the walk are shown on the route maps, and in the information. Allow more time if it has been wet, if you are elderly, or have children or inexperienced walkers with you. Also bear in mind that a steep ascent or crossing a large, recently ploughed, field can slow you up considerably.

The route has been established in consultation with landowners and farmers and follows public rights of way and permissive paths. Remember that most public paths cross private estates and farmland. Some evolved as routes from farms to the nearest village and were not designed for large numbers

of people. Often you are walking through a place of work; enjoy the countryside but please have regard for its life and work. Crops and animals are the farmers' livelihood and should be left undisturbed.

Always keep to the path to avoid trespass and walk in single file through a crop. Report any obstructions or other problems to the appropriate Highway Authority, East Sussex or Kent County Council (see page 65)

Like most long-distance walks the Wealdway unavoidably uses the occasional country lane, where in general traffic is only light. Nevertheless, by their very nature, lanes tend to be narrow and wind with blind bends. Therefore walkers must be vigilant at all times by keeping an adequate line of sight in both directions for passing vehicles. This does not mean always keeping to the right to face the traffic because on a tight bend turning to the right, there may not be enough space or time for a driver to see you and take avoiding action. Well before a right-hand bend, and when it is safe to do so, cross to the other side where there is a clearer line of sight. Crossing at the bend can be very dangerous. If you happen to be on the left side when approaching a left-hand bend, again cross to the right well before the bend. Thus a greater and clearer line of sight is achieved and there is less chance of being hit from behind by a vehicle hugging the left-hand verge. In a group of two or

more, always walk in single file.

Remember to leave things as found – refasten gates you find closed. Straying stock can cause damage and an expensive inconvenience to farmers. Always use gates and stiles to negotiate fences and hedges.

Carry your litter until it can be disposed of in a proper bin. Litter, including orange peel and banana skins, is unsightly and can spoil other people's pleasure; it can also be dangerous and can injure people, animals and wildlife. Guard against all risk of fire, especially in dry weather.

Although you may stop briefly to take refreshment, formal picnicking is not permitted on private land; you only have a right of passage on a right of way.

To avoid injury or distress to farm animals and wildlife, keep dogs under control at all times. If not on a lead they can run surprisingly long distances and consequently may be out of sight and the control of the owner. Please keep dogs on leads, particularly when passing through fruit growing areas, fields with standing crops or livestock, heathland and woodlands. Farmers have a right to shoot dogs found worrying their livestock.

> *They only know a country who are acquainted with its footpaths. By the roads, indeed, the outside may be seen; but the footpaths go through the heart of the land.*
> Richard Jeffries

River Medway

Country Code

Enjoy the countryside and respect its life and work

– * –

Guard against all risk of fire

– * –

Leave all gates as found

– * –

Keep your dogs under close control

– * –

Keep to public paths across farmland

– * –

Use gates and stiles to negotiate fences, hedges and walls

– * –

Leave livestock, crops and machinery alone

– * –

Take your litter home

– * –

Help to keep all water clean

– * –

Protect wildlife, plants and trees

– * –

Take special care on country roads

– * –

Make no unnecessary noise

First aid kit

You can vary its contents for the type of walking and length of time you are away. The items listed provide a comprehensive first aid kit; try to include at least one of each and make sure you know how to deal with common injuries such as stings, sprains and minor cuts.

– * –

❑ Plasters
❑ Sterile wound dressing
❑ Crepe bandage
❑ Triangular bandage
❑ Antiseptic cream and wipes
❑ Insect repellent cream
❑ Sting relief
❑ Aspirin/ Paracetamol
❑ Scissors
❑ Safety pins
❑ Tweezers

Kit for the walk

THE WEALDWAY is never far from civilisation and is suitable even for family groups and the occasional rambler, since it can be tackled in short stages, without elaborate walking gear. However you will need some basic kit.

Always wear suitable clothing and footwear for the season. Be prepared for changeable weather. Take clothes which are warm and waterproof.

Sections of paths may be muddy after periods of rain, so wear strong, comfortable and waterproof footwear. Light boots are by far the best but whatever footwear you use make sure that it is 'worn-in' and that it has an adequate tread.

Don't leave your waterproofs behind to skimp on weight. Nothing is more miserable than being caught out in an unexpected storm. Inexpensive overtrousers will give protection

Kit Check List

For a day's walk you will need:

❑ Wealdway guidebook
❑ Strong shoes, preferably boots
❑ Comfortable rucksack
❑ Waterproof jacket with hood, or hat, overtrousers and possibly gaiters
❑ Food and drink
❑ Bus/train timetable(s)
❑ Camera and spare film
❑ Binoculars
❑ Pocket knife
❑ First-aid kit (*see bottom left*)
❑ Watch
❑ Wallet, purse and cash
❑ Pen/pencil
❑ Sweater/pullover (*if cold*)
❑ Hat, gloves and scarf (*for winter walking*)
❑ Handkerchief
❑ Sun glasses/ sun block cream
❑ Water container

These days many walkers carry mobile 'phones. They provide reassurance in terms of safety and convenience.

– * –

For a walk of more than a day's duration you will also need:

❑ Spare walking socks
❑ Spare clothes and light footwear
❑ Night clothes
❑ Toiletries
❑ Towel

from any discomfort caused by walking through high vegetation or rain-drenched crops. Gaiters, even short ankle ones, may not be stylish but they stop trousers and socks getting soaked or muddy.

It is important that your rucksack is comfortable and can hold the items you wish to carry. Avoid shoulder bags as they do not spread the weight evenly, can cause aches and swing, thereby throwing you off-balance when crossing a stile, for example. Try also to avoid small rucksacks; they may look light but they too can cause aches because the carrying straps put a strain on your shoulders. A good rucksack, properly fitted to your hips with a waist belt, will carry a reasonable weight in comfort.

Finally, don't forget to leave a note of your whereabouts, especially if you intend to walk alone.

Using the guidebook

THIS BOOK IS DESIGNED to be both an area travel guide and a practical guide to walking the Wealdway in either direction. It is a guidebook containing a route guide. It may be used intact or separately by carefully removing the weather-resistant route guide from the centre of the book, by pulling the middle staple out. The guidebook contains a travelogue, specialist and other information and guidance on planning and preparing for a walk. The route guide, with information about features passed en route, is self-contained and can be used on the walk independently of the guidebook.

The route maps have been arranged in sequence from Eastbourne to Gravesend. When walking from south to north the two sections are used in a conventional way, whilst the north to south route is read from the last page of each section to the first. Either way the presentation is clear and the route is easily followed.

The route maps are arranged in sequence from south to north because it makes following the maps easier. With the north point at the top of each page the maps are aligned the same way you are walking. It is also more comfortable walking northwards since the sun and the prevailing wind are behind you from the south-west. Remember though, that in the fickleness of British weather, you may get a cold north-east wind blowing in from the North Sea.

Which way to walk?

As with any long-distance walk the question arises: which way should it be walked? In the end the choice to walk north or south is probably a matter of temperament, as either way leads you over open hilltops and through quiet pastoral scenery, timeless villages and lonely fields. The maps in this guide run from Eastbourne to Gravesend, for ease of reading and the trek northwards to the Thames

estuary has many attractions, including the comfort of having the elements generally at one's back. But scenically the climax of the walk is at its southern end – the great whale-backed down which plunges to the sea in the cliffs of Beachy Head. The walk southwards across the Weald to the English Channel, with glimpses towards it from the heathy heights of Ashdown, is an exhilarating experience, as each intricate valley and little hill leads nearer to southern England's highest sea cliffs.

By carefully folding it back, the guidebook and/or route guide will fit into a map case, thus providing protection against damage, dirt and damp.

Route options

THE WEALDWAY is 82 miles (131.2kms) long or 83½ miles (133.6km) via the Beachy Head loop and can be undertaken as a long-distance walk in about a week, six days, approximately 13½ miles (21.6km) each. If your walk is continuous, you may wish to consider extra days for rest and exploration in nearby places of interest, for example Royal Tunbridge Wells.

The walk can be undertaken in sections or shorter walks can be devised, of a day or half-day's duration, depending on your ability and time

Distance checklist

This chart will assist you in calculating the distances between places on the Wealdway, planning overnight stops or checking your progress along the walk. All distances are approximate.

| | Distance from previous location | | Accumulative distance | |
Location	miles	km	miles	km
Eastbourne	0	0.0	0	0.0
Jevington	7	11.2	7	11.2
Wilmington	3½	5.6	10½	16.8
Arlington	2½	4.0	13	20.8
Upper Dicker	1¾	2.8	14¾	23.6
Upper Horsebridge	2½	4.0	17¼	27.6
Hellingly	1	1.6	18¼	29.2
Chiddingly	3¼	5.2	21½	34.4
East Hoathly	2	3.2	23½	37.6
Blackboys	4	6.4	27½	44.0
Uckfield	2¾	4.4	30¼	48.1
Fairwarp	4	6.4	34¼	54.8
Camp Hill	2¼	3.6	36½	58.4
Withyham	4¾	7.6	41¼	66.0
Stone Cross	3¾	6.0	45	72.0
Fordcombe	1	1.6	46	73.6
Speldhurst	2	3.2	48	76.8
Bidborough	2¼	3.6	50¼	80.4
Haysden	2	3.2	52¼	83.6
Tonbridge	2	3.2	54¼	86.8
Barnes Street	4¾	7.6	59	94.4
West Peckham	3¾	6.0	62¾	100.4
Platt	4¼	6.8	67	107.2
Wrotham Heath	1	1.6	68	108.8
Great Buckland	5¼	8.4	73¼	117.2
Luddesdown	1½	2.4	74¾	119.6
Sole Street	1½	2.4	76¼	122.0
Tollgate	3¾	5.2	79½	127.2
Gravesend	2½	4.0	82	131.2

availability, using the bus and train routes which link with many of the places along the route (look for the bus and rail symbols on the route maps and the transport map on page 64 of the route guide).

If you wish to undertake the Wealdway in sections or as a series of short walks you need to be aware of problems of returning to your starting point. Possible solutions might be as follows:

- Using two cars, one at the starting point and the other at the proposed finishing point.
- Using one car and public transport. If relying on infrequent bus services it is suggested that you make your outward journey by bus, thus returning confidently to your car or base.
- Retracing your steps. The scenery can look surprisingly different when walking in the opposite direction.

Maps

Ordnance Survey sheet numbers and titles:

Explorer Series

Scale 1:25,000 – 2¹/₂ inches to 1 mile (4cm to 1km)

These maps are the replacements for the Pathfinder series which is being phased out. With larger area coverage, these highly detailed maps clearly depict the rights of way network as well as showing selected tourist information. The perfect walking companion, they are ideal if you want to devise your own walks in the area.

Landranger Series

Scale 1:50,000 – 1¹/₄ inches to 1 mile (2cm to 1km). These all-purpose maps include selected tourist information, caravan and camping sites, picnic areas, view points and rights of way.

199 Eastbourne & Hastings, Battle & Heathfield
198 Brighton & The Downs
188 Maidstone & The Weald of Kent
177 East London, Billericay & Gravesend

123 South Downs Way, Newhaven to Eastbourne
135 Ashdown Forest
147 Sevenoaks & Tonbridge
136 The Weald, Royal Tunbridge Wells
148 Maidstone & the Medway Towns
163 Gravesend & Rochester

To obtain the most up-to-date information on the maps available and for further information on Ordnance Survey maps and guides contact Customer Information,

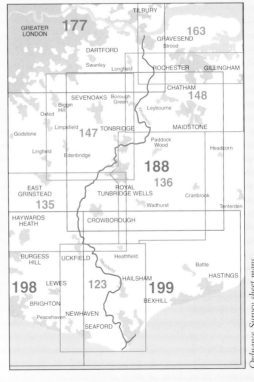

Ordnance Survey sheet maps

Ordnance Survey, Romsey Road, Southampton, SO16 4GU, ☎ (0345) 33 00 11.
  Ordnance Survey maps covering the Wealdway are available from bookshops, local tourist information centres and the Support

Services Officer, Environmental Management Unit, Strategic Planning Directorate, Kent County Council, Invicta House, County Hall, Maidstone, Kent ME14 1XX, ☎ (01622) 221526.

Grid references

The grid references of the starting and finishing points of each section of the route of the Wealdway are given in the route guide.

The framework of squares spaced at one kilometre intervals over Ordnance Survey maps is known as the National Grid. The grid facilitates the pinpointing of any place in the country, giving it a unique reference number.

Eastings
To give a reference number, first take the western (left-hand) edge of the kilometre square in which the place lies. Read the figures at the end of the line at either the top or bottom margins of the map, then moving eastwards (to the right) estimate the position of the place in tenths across the square.

Northings Secondly, take the southern edge of the map square and read the figures at the end of the line at either the left or right side margins of the map. Then, moving northwards, estimate the position of the place in tenths up the square. This gives the place a six figure reference number accurate to within 100 metres.

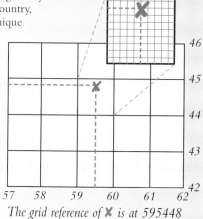

The grid reference of ✖ *is at 595448*

In finding out a grid reference, the first three numbers of the six figure number refer to the line and number of tenths across the square, whilst the second three numbers refer to the line and number of tenths up the square.

Waymarking and signing

THE TERM WAYMARKING refers to marking objects along a public right of way. It complements signposting, which shows where a right of way leaves the metalled road and indicates its initial direction, and enables users to follow a path accurately and confidently at points where they might otherwise have difficulty.

Waymarking benefits not only users of rights of way but also farmers and landowners. It increases users' enjoyment of the countryside and helps to prevent unintentional trespass.

Wealdway badges

Wealdway badges can be obtained from the **Wealdway Steering Group,** *c/o Dr Ben Perkins, 11 Old London Road, Brighton, East Sussex BN1 8XR.*

Waymarking system

The recommended system in England and Wales uses small coloured arrows to show the direction of the path and also to act as a target when viewed from a distance. A different colour is used for each category of right of way.

If the status of a path changes along its length, so does the colour of the waymarking arrows. Where a right of way is part of a special route, such as a National Trail, Recreation Route or Circular Walk, the arrows are used in conjunction with the route's own symbol.

Public rights of way that are the footpaths are waymarked using yellow arrows.

Bridleways are waymarked with blue arrows.

Byways open to all traffic are waymarked with red arrows, but they are intended only to show the status of the route and not indicate whether it is physically suitable for vehicles.

63

Transport

Car parking Places to park are shown on the route maps. Please note that these are not necessarily car parks. Please park thoughtfully and sensibly if a car park is not available, to avoid causing an obstruction (at a gate, or farm access, for example) or damage to the roadside verges. Leave your car securely locked with valuables out of sight.

Bus and train services It is not practical to give details of all the bus and train routes and services to and along the Wealdway, since they may change during the life of this guidebook.

For information about all bus and train services in East Sussex, contact Riders Services, Transport & Environment Department, East Sussex County Council, County Hall, St Anne's Crescent, Lewes, East Sussex BN7 1UE, ☎ (01273) 474747.

Kent County Council publishes an annual Public Transport Map and Guide which contains comprehensive bus and rail route maps and lists of bus services and operators. Public transport information can be obtained from Commercial Services, Kent County Council, Gibson Drive, Kings Hill, West Malling, Kent, ME19 4QG, ☎ (08457) 696996.

For details of train services please telephone either (0345) 48 49 50 or (0171) 928 5100.

You are advised to check details of your journey before travelling, particularly on Sundays.

Transport map

Accommodation

THERE ARE ADEQUATE bed and breakfast establishments along the Wealdway (look for the bed symbols on the route maps). It is advisable to book accommodation in advance, especially in the summer.

A comprehensive *Wealdway Accommodation Guide* (£2.50) can be obtained from either the Rights of Way Section, Transport & Environment Department, East Sussex County Council, County Hall, St Anne's Crescent, Lewes, East Sussex BN7 1UE, ☎ (01273) 482250, the Support Services Officer, Environmental Management Unit, Strategic Planning Directorate, Kent County Council, Invicta House, County Hall, Maidstone, Kent ME14 1XX, ☎ (01622) 221526, or the Wealdway Steering Group, c/o Dr Ben Perkins, 11 Old London Road, Brighton, East Sussex BN1 8XR, ☎ (01273) 883306.

Information about accommodation along the Wealdway can be obtained from the following organisations:
East Sussex Tourism
Contact local tourist information offices
Kent Tourism
Economic Development Unit, Strategic Planning Directorate, Kent County Council, Invicta House, County Hall, Maidstone, Kent ME14 1XX,
☎ (01622) 696165
South East England Tourist Board and Eastbourne, Hailsham, Boship Roundabout, Royal Tunbridge Wells, Tonbridge and Gravesend Tourist Information Centres and Uckfield Town Council (listed on page 65).

Ramblers' Association

The Ramblers' Association (for address see page 65) publishes the Ramblers' Year Book and Accommodation Guide, which is available from local bookshops.

Youth Hostels

There are three youth hostels close to the Wealdway:

Youth Hostels Association
Trevelyan House, 8 St Stephens Hill, St Albans, Hertfordshire, AL1 2DY, ☎ (01727) 845047.

Eastbourne (½ mile, 0.8km) (TV 588990), Youth Hostel, East Dean Road, Eastbourne, East Sussex BN20 8ES, ☎ (01323) 721081.

Alfriston (2½ miles, 4km) (TQ 518019), Youth Hostel, Frog Firle, Alfriston, Polegate, East Sussex BN26 5TT, ☎ (01323) 870423.

Blackboys (1 mile, 1.6km) (TQ 521215), Youth Hostel, Blackboys, Uckfield, East Sussex TN22 5HU, ☎ (01825) 890607.

You may join the Youth Hostels Association on arrival at the hostel but prior booking is advisable.

Useful contacts

IF YOU HAVE any comments or suggestions about this or any other recreation route in East Sussex please contact Rights of Way and Countryside Management Service, Transport & Environment Department, East Sussex County Council, County Hall, St Anne's Crescent, Lewes, East Sussex BN7 1UE, ☎ (01273) 482250 or 481654.

In Kent please contact the Support Services Officer, Environmental Management Unit, Strategic Planning Directorate, Kent County Council, Invicta House, County Hall, Maidstone, Kent ME14 1XX, ☎ (01622) 221526.

The route should not be obstructed in any way but if it is in East Sussex please contact the following organisations: Between Eastbourne (Beachy Head) and the A27 road, Sussex Downs Conservation Board, Seven Sisters Country Park, Exceat, Seaford, East Sussex BN25 4AD, ☎ (01323) 870280; for the remainder, Rights of Way Section, Transport & Environment Department, East Sussex County Council, County Hall, St Anne's Cresecent, Lewes, East Sussex BN7 1UE, ☎ (01273) 482250.

In Kent please contact the Rights of Way Manager, Environmental Management Unit, Strategic Planning Directorate, Kent County Council, Invicta House, County Hall, Maidstone, Kent ME14 1XX, ☎ (01622) 221513.

Tourist information

South East England Tourist Board: The Old Brew House, Warwick Park, Royal Tunbridge Wells, Kent TN2 5TU, ☎ (01892) 540766.

Eastbourne: Tourist Information Centre, 3 Cornfield Road, Eastbourne, East Sussex BN21 4QL, ☎ (01323) 411400.

Hailsham: Tourist Information Centre, The Library, Western Road, Hailsham, East Sussex BN27 3DN, ☎ (01323) 844426.

Boship Roundabout (A22 road): Tourist Information Centre, Boship Roundabout (A22 road), Lower Dicker, East Sussex BN27 4DP, ☎ (01323) 442667.

Uckfield: Uckfield Town Council, Uckfield Civic Centre, Belfarm Lane, Uckfield, East Sussex TN22 1AE, ☎ (01825) 762774.

Royal Tunbridge Wells: Tourist Information Centre, The Old Fishmarket, The Pantiles, Royal Tunbridge Wells, Kent TN2 5TN, ☎ (01892) 515675.

Tonbridge: Tourist Information Centre, Tonbridge Castle, Castle Street, Tonbridge, Kent TN9 1BG, ☎ (01732) 770929.

Gravesend: Tourist Information Centre, 10 Parrock Street, Gravesend, Kent DA12 1ET, ☎ (01474) 337600.

Walkers' organisations

Ramblers' Association 1/5 Wandsworth Road, London SW8 2XX, ☎ (0171) 339 8500.

Sussex Area Secretary Mrs Janet Barber, 7 Stirling Way, Horsham, West Sussex, RH13 5RX, ☎ (01403) 263346.

Kent Area Secretary Mr Peter Skipp, 81 New Street Hill, Bromley, Kent BR1 5BA.

Long Distance Walkers' Association *General Secretary,* Mr Les Maple, 1 Upcroft, Windsor, Berkshire SL4 3NH, ☎ (01753) 866685.

East Sussex Area Secretary Mr Tony Carter, 54 Dover Road, Polegate, East Sussex BN26 6LG, ☎ (01323) 484211.

Kent Area Secretary Mr D Sheldrake, 26 Highview, Vigo Village, Meopham, Gravesend, Kent DA13 0RR, ☎ (01732) 823643.

Conservation bodies

Sussex Wildlife Trust Woods Mill, Henfield, West Sussex BN5 9SD, ☎ (01273) 492630.

Kent Wildlife Trust Tyland Barn, Sandling, Maidstone, Kent ME14 3BD, ☎ (01622) 662012.

Countryside Agency South East Regional Office, 4th floor, 71 Kingsway, London WC2B 6ST, ☎ (0171) 831 3510.

Sussex Downs Conservation Board, Seven Sisters Country Park, Exceat, Seaford, East Sussex BN25 4AD, ☎ (01323) 870280.

High Weald Unit Corner Farm, Hastings Road, Flimwell, East Sussex TN5 7PR, ☎ (01580) 879500.

Kent High Weald Project Council Offices, High Street, Cranbrook, Kent TN17 3EN, ☎ (01580) 712771.

Miscellaneous

Ordnance Survey Romsey Road, Maybush, Southampton, Hampshire SO9 4DH, ☎ (01730) 792000.

Weathercall, (up-to-date weather forecast), East Sussex & Kent Area, ☎ (0891) 772272

Exploring the *area*

> 66 *We shall not cease from exploration*
> *And the end of all our exploring*
> *Will be to arrive where we started*
> *And know the place for the first time* 99
> T S Eliot

Interesting places to visit on, or near, the *Wealdway*

Musgrave Collection
131 Royal Parade, Eastbourne
☎ (01323) 648106

Eastbourne Butterfly Centre
Royal Parade, Eastbourne
☎ (01323) 645522

Redoubt Fortress
Royal Parade, Eastbourne
☎ (01323) 410300

Eastbourne Pier
☎ (01323) 410466

'How we lived then'
Museum of shops
20 Cornfield Terrace,
Eastbourne
☎ (01323) 737143

Wish Tower
Eastbourne, ☎ (01323)
410440 or (0424) 434299

RNLI Lifeboat Museum
Eastbourne
☎ (01323) 730717

Eastbourne Heritage Centre
2 Carlisle Road, Eastbourne
☎ (01323) 411189/509406

Towner Museum & Art Gallery
High Street, Old Town,
Eastbourne
☎ (01323) 411688

Combe Hill neolithic camp
near Jevington

Filching Manor &
Motor Museum
Jevington Road,
Wannock
☎ (01323) 487838/487124

Long Man of Wilmington
near Wilmington

Clergy House
Alfriston
☎ (01323) 870001

Alfriston Heritage
Centre & Blacksmiths
☎ (01323) 870303

Drusillas
near Alfriston
☎ (01323) 870324
information & (01323)
870656 bookings

Michelham Priory
Michelham
☎ (01323) 844224

Bentley Wildfowl Reserve
& Motor Museum
Bentley Farm, Halland
☎ (01825) 840573

Sussex Farm Museum
Horam Manor Estate,
Horam
☎ (01435) 32597

St George's Vineyard
Waldron
☎ (01435) 32156

Bridge Cottage
Uckfield
☎ (01825) 762632

Barnsgate Manor Vineyard
Heron's Ghyll
☎ (01825) 713366

Ashdown Forest Centre
Wych Cross
☎ (01342) 823583

Nutley Windmill
☎ (01825) 762969

Pooh Sticks Bridge
near Hartfield
☎ (01892) 770453

Pooh Corner
High Street, Hartfield
☎ (01892) 770453

Groombridge Place Gardens
☎ (01892) 863999

Penshurst Place and Gardens
☎ (01892) 870307

Penshurst Vineyards
Grove Road, Penshurst
☎ (01892) 890286

David Salomon's House
Southborough
☎ (01892) 515152

The Pantiles & the Bath House
Royal Tunbridge Wells
☎ (01892) 548861

'A Day at the Wells'
The Corn Exchange,
Royal Tunbridge Wells
☎ (01892) 546545

Museum & Art Gallery
Mount Pleasant Road,
Royal Tunbridge Wells
☎ (01892) 526121

Tonbridge Castle
☎ (01732) 770929

Hop Farm Country Park
Beltring
☎ (01622) 872068

Old Soar Manor
Plaxtol
☎ (01892) 890651

Ightam Mote
Ivy Hatch
☎ (01732) 810378

Great Comp Garden
Platt
☎ (01732) 883889

Nepicar Farm
Wrotham Heath
☎ (01732) 883040

Meopham Windmill
Meopham Green
☎ (01474) 812110

Coldrum Stones long barrow
near Trottiscliffe

Yeoman's House
Sole Street,
DA12 3AX
Viewed by written
application to tenant.

Cobham Hall
Cobham
☎ (01474) 824319/823371

Owletts
Cobham
☎ (01892) 890651

St Andrews Arts Centre
Gravesend
☎ (01474) 337600

St George's Church
& the statue
of Pocahontas
Gravesend
☎ (01474) 534965

Chantry Heritage Centre
Fort Gardens,
Gravesend
☎ (01474) 321520

New Tavern Fort
Fort Gardens,
Gravesend
☎ (01474) 536995

Parish Churches
Key usually
obtained
locally if
not open.

Countryside open spaces *on, or near, the Wealdway*

Eastbourne downland (including Beachy Head & Belle Tout)
Eastbourne
☎ (01323) 410000

Seven Sisters Country Park
Exceat, Seaford
☎ (01323) 870100

Friston Forest
between Exceat,
Alfriston and Jevington

Lullington Heath
East Sussex National
Nature Reserves, between
Alfriston and Jevington
☎ (01273) 476595

Abbots Wood and Abbots Wood Trail,
Arlington,
☎ (01323) 870911

Arlington Reservoir
Fishing Lodge, Arlington
☎ (01323) 870810

Ashdown Forest
Ashdown Forest Centre,
Wych Cross
☎ (01342) 823583

Harrison's Rocks
Groombridge
☎ (01892) 864238

Southborough Common
Southborough,
Royal Tunbridge Wells
☎ (01892) 529176

High Rocks
High Rocks Lane,
Royal Tunbridge Wells
☎ (01892) 526074

Rusthall Common & the Toad Rock
Rusthall,
Royal Tunbridge Wells
☎ (01892) 526121

Royal Tunbridge Wells Common & Wellington Rocks
☎ (01892) 526121

Haysden Country Park
Lower Hayesden Lane,
Tonbridge
☎ (01732) 844522

Trosley Country Park
near Trottiscliffe
☎ (01732) 823570

Camer Country Park
Meopham
☎ (01474) 337489/
337575

St Peter's Church, Folkington

67

Other walking opportunities

KENT has 4,273 miles (6,837km) of Public Rights of Way to enjoy. Kent County Council is committed to maintaining and promoting access across the county for residents and visitors. Working with our partner organisations, over 600 miles (960km) have been waymarked as Kent County Council recreation routes.

In East Sussex you will find a varied landscape ranging from chalk downland to the ridges and steep valleys of the High Weald, all served by a network of over 2,200 miles (3,520km) of public paths. There are many opportunities to explore this well-maintained network and discover quiet, secluded countryside.

If you have enjoyed this walk and would like to explore other waymarked walking routes in East Sussex, write to Rights of Way and Countryside Management Service, Transport and Environment Department, East Sussex County Council, County Hall, St Anne's Cresecent, Lewes, East Sussex BN7 1UE and in Kent write to the Support Services Officer, Environmental Management Unit, Strategic Planning Directorate, Kent County Council, Invicta House, County Hall, Maidstone, Kent ME14 1XX, ☎ (01622) 221526.

It is possible for you to devise your own shorter linear and circular walks using the extensive rights of way network throughout the counties. Information about these can be obtained by studying either the Ordnance Survey Explorer maps or the East Sussex and Kent County Council Definitive Maps of Public Rights of Way. Copies of the latter can be inspected at public libraries or district council offices. In the event of difficulty please contact the Public Rights of Way Units in either East Sussex or Kent County Councils (see page 65). Linked, or running close, to the Wealdway are a number of other walks, as follows:

1066 Country Walk

Inspired by the historical events of 1066, the walk runs for 31 miles (49.6km) between Rye and Pevensey Castle via Battle Abbey, with links to the South Downs Way at Jevington. *1066 Country Walk* (leaflet) – Rother District Council, Town Hall, Bexhill-on-Sea, East Sussex TN39 3JX.

Cuckoo Trail

Formerly a railway line, the Cuckoo trail is a safe and attractive route for walkers and cyclists. The ten-mile (16km) route takes in the countryside between Polegate and Heathfield. *Cuckoo Trail* (leaflet) – Wealden District Council, Council Offices, Pine Grove, Crowborough, East Sussex TN6 1DH

Eden Valley Walk

A 15-mile (24km) walk along the valleys of the River Eden and River Medway between Edenbridge and Tonbridge. Passing through the High Weald it takes in the historic castles and houses at Hever, Chiddingstone and Penshurst. *Eden Valley Walk* (booklet) – Kent County Council, Strategic Planning Directorate, Invicta House, County Hall, Maidstone, Kent ME14 1XX.

Forest Way

The Way has been developed as a linear country park along the trackbed of a former branch railway between East Grinstead and Ashurst junction, Groombridge. It runs along the upper Medway valley. *The Forest Way Country Park and Circular Walks* (leaflet)

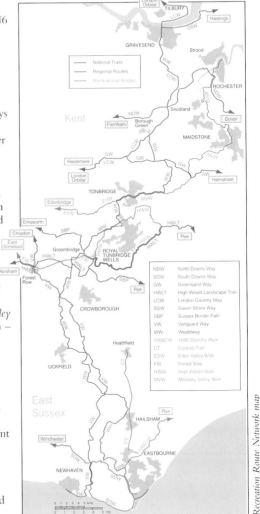

Recreation Route Network map

– Rights of Way and Countryside Management Service, Transport and Environment Department, East Sussex County Council, County Hall, St Anne's Crescent, Lewes, East Sussex BN7 1UE.

Greensand Way

A walk along the Greensand hills of Surrey and Kent between Haslemere and Hamstreet. The 108-mile (172.8km) walk follows the Greensand ridge through a varied landscape of heathland, woodland, orchards and hop gardens.

Greensand Way (book) – Surrey County Council, Environment Department, County Hall, Kingston-upon-Thames, Surrey KT1 2DY and Kent County Council, Strategic Planning Directorate, Invicta House, County Hall, Maidstone, Kent ME14 1XX.

High Weald Landscape Trail

Running for 89 miles (142.4km) between Horsham and Rye, through the unique landscape of the High Weald, the centre of the 16th-century iron industry, the trail takes in hop gardens, orchards, villages and historic gardens.

High Weald Landscape Trail (book) – High Weald AONB Unit, Corner Farm, Hastings Road, Flimwell, East Sussex TN5 7PR.

High Weald Walk

A 28-mile (44.8km) circular walk in the High Weald around Royal Tunbridge Wells with link routes from the town centre. The

walk passes through a rolling landscape of ridges and valleys.

High Weald Walk (booklet) – Kent County Council, Strategic Planning Directorate, Invicta House, County Hall, Maidstone, Kent ME14 1XX.

London Country Walk

A complete walk circuit of 206 miles (329.6km) around London keeping between 13 and 31 miles (20.8 and 9.6km) from its centre. The Way passes through the varied landscape of the home counties; woodland, heathland, canals, rivers, chalk and sandstone hills.

Guide to the London Countryway (book) – Constable and Co Ltd, 3 The Lanchesters, 162 Fulham Palace Road, London W6 9ER.

Medway Valley Walk

A valley walk running for 28 miles (44.8km) between Tonbridge and Rochester through a varied landscape of downland, woodland, orchards and hop gardens, meadows and farmland, lakes and marshland, and unspoilt villages and historic towns.

Medway Valley Walk (book) – Kent County Council, Strategic Planning Directorate, Invicta House, County Hall, Maidstone, Kent ME14 1XX.

North Downs Way

The National Trail (142 miles, 227.2km) broadly follows the historic Pilgrims' Way between Farnham and Dover with an

alternative loop via Canterbury. Except for the first 14 miles (22.4km), the trail follows the North Downs on or just below the escarpment.

North Downs Way (book) – Aurum Press, 25 Bedford Avenue, London WC1B 3AT.

North Downs Way: A Practical Handbook (booklet) – Kent County Council, Strategic Planning Directorate, Invicta House, County Hall, Maidstone, Kent ME14 1XX.

National Trails in the South East of England (leaflet) – Countryside Agency Postal Sales, PO Box 124, Walgrave, Northampton NN6 9TL.

Saxon Shore Way

Running for 163 miles (260.8km) around the ancient coastline between Gravesend and Hastings, the Way follows the marshland of the Thames and Medway estuaries, the White Cliffs of Dover and the old sea cliffs overlooking Romney Marsh.

Saxon Shore Way (book) – Aurum Press, 25 Bedford Avenue, London WC1B 3AT

South Downs Way

This National Trail follows the escarpment of the South Downs for 101 miles (161.6km) between Eastbourne and Winchester, with an alternative loop via Beachy Head to Alfriston, affording views across the Weald and the sea.

South Downs Way (book) – Aurum Press, 25 Bedford Avenue, London WC1B 3AT

South Downs Way strip-map (map) – Harvey Maps, 12-16 Main Street, Donne, Perthshire FK16 6BJ.

Accommodation Guide to the South Downs Way (booklet) – South Downs Way Officer, Sussex Downs Conservation Board, Chanctonbury House, Church Street, Storrington, West Sussex RH20 4LT.

National Trails in the South East of England (leaflet) – Countryside Agency Postal Sales, PO Box 124, Walgrave, Northampton NN6 9TL.

Sussex Border Path

The 152-mile (243.2km) route, between Emsworth and Rye, follows paths approximating to the Sussex border with Hampshire, Surrey and Kent, through the South Downs and the Weald.

Sussex Border Path (pack) – Dr Ben Perkins, 11 Old London Road, Brighton, Sussex BN1 8XR.

Vanguard Way

The Way, from the suburbs of London to the sea, runs for 55 miles (88km) between East Croydon and Newhaven. It crosses the North and South Downs and Ashdown Forest in the Weald.

Vanguard Way (booklet) – Vanguards Rambling Club, c/o 109 Selsdon Park Road, South Croydon, CR2 8JJ

Further information and references

Bibliography

- *Archaeologia Cantiana*
  Various volumes
- *Buildings of England (The): Sussex*
  Ian Nairn & Nikolaus Pevsner
  Penguin
- *Buildings of England (The), West Kent and The Weald*
  John Newman
  Penguin
- *Classic Landforms of the Weald*
  D A Robinson & R B G Williams
  The Geographical Association
- *East Sussex*
  Keith Spence
  Philips
- *East Sussex*
  W S Mitchell
  Shell
- *Exploring Kent Churches*
  John E Vigar
  Meresborough Books
- *Exploring Sussex Churches*
  John E Vigar
  Meresborough Books
- *Highways and Byways in Kent*
  Walter Jerrold
  Macmillan
- *Highways and Byways in Sussex*
  E V Lucas
  Macmillan
- *History of Kent (A)*
  Frank W Jessup
  Phillimore

- *History of Sussex (A)*
  J R Armstrong
  Phillimore
- *Iron Industry of the Weald (The)*
  H Cleere & D Crossley
  Leicester University Press
- *Journey through the Weald*
  Ben Darby
  Hale
- *Kent*
  Marcus Crouch
  Batsford
- *Kent*
  Roger Higham
  Batsford
- *Kent*
  Pennethorne Hughes
  Shell
- *King's England, Kent (The)*
  Arthur Mee
  Hodder and Stoughton
- *King's England, Sussex (The)*
  Arthur Mee
  Hodder and Stoughton
- *Portrait of Ashdown Forest*
  Roger Penn
  Hale
- *Portrait of the River Medway*
  Roger Penn
  Hale
- *Roman Ways in the Weald*
  I D Margary
  Phoenix House
- *Shire County Guide: Kent*
  John E Vigar
  Shire Publications
- *South East England*
  Richard Wyndham
  Batsford

- *Sussex*
  Barbara Willard
  Batsford
- *Sussex*
  John Burke
  Batsford
- *Sussex Archaeological Collections*
  Various volumes
- *Sussex Landscape (The)*
  Peter Brandon
  Hodder and Stoughton
- *Sussex Pottery*
  J M Baines
  Fisher Publications
- *Visitors Guide to Kent (The)*
  Kev Reynolds
  Moorland Publishing
- *Visitor's Guide to Sussex (The)*
  Jim Cleland
  Moorland Publishing
- *Walk Around Gravesend Town Centre (A)*
  Impact
  Gravesham Borough Council
- *Weald (The)*
  W Gibbons
  Unwin
- *Weald (The)*
  S W Wooldridge & F Goldring
  Collins
- *Weald of Kent and Sussex*
  Sheila Kaye-Smith
  Robert Hale
- *Wilmington Giant (The)*
  Rodney Castleden
  Turnstone Press

Table of Architectural Periods

	Romanesque	1066–1190
Gothic	Early English	1190–1280
	Decorated	1280–1380
	Perpendicular	1380–1550
	Classical	1550–1810
	Gothic & Classical Revival	1810–1914
	Modern	1914–present day

Countryside Access Charter

Your rights of way are:

- *Public footpaths* – on foot only
- *Bridleway* – on foot, horseback and pedal cycle.
- *Byways* – (usually old roads), most roads used as public paths and, of course *public roads* – all traffic.

Use maps, signs and waymarks. Ordnance Survey Explorer and Landranger maps show most public rights of way.

On rights of way you can:

- Take a pram, pushchair or wheelchair if practicable.
- Take a dog (on a lead or under close control).
- Take a short route round an illegal obstruction or remove it sufficiently to get past.

You have a right to go for recreation to:

- Public parks and open spaces – on foot.
- Most commons near older towns and cities – on foot and sometimes on horseback.
- Private land where the owner has a formal agreement with the local authority.

In addition you can use the following by local or established custom or consent:

- Many areas of open country like moorland, fell and coastal areas, especially those of the National Trust, and most commons.
- Some woods and forests, especially those owned by the Forestry Commission and the Woodland Trust.
- Country parks and picnic sites.
- Most beaches.
- Towpaths on canals and rivers.
- Some land that is being rested from agriculture, where notices allowing access are displayed.
- Some private paths and tracks. Consent sometimes extends to riding horses and pedal cycles. *Ask for advice if you are unsure.*

For your information

- County and metropolitan district councils and London boroughs have a duty to protect, maintain and record rights of way, and hold registers of commons and village greens – report problems you find on them.
- Obstructions, dangerous animals, harassment and misleading signs on rights of way are illegal.
- If a public path runs along the edge of a field, it must not be ploughed or disturbed.
- A public path across a field can be ploughed or disturbed to cultivate a crop, but the surface must be quickly restored and the line of the path made apparent on the ground.
- Crops (other than grass) must not be allowed to inconvenience the use of a rights of way, or prevent the line from being apparent on the ground.
- Landowners can require you to leave land to which you have no right of access.
- Motor vehicles are normally permitted only on roads, byways and some roads used as public paths.
- Follow any local bylaws.

And, wherever you go, follow the Country Code (see page 60)

This Charter is for practical guidance in England and Wales only. Fuller advice is given in a free booklet 'Out in the Country' available from the Countryside Agency Postal Sales, PO Box 124, Walgrave, Northampton NN6 9TL, ☎ (01604) 781848. Published with kind permission of the Countryside Agency.

Table of Historical Periods

Prehistoric	Mesolithic		10000–3500BC
	Neolithic		3500–2000BC
	Bronze Age		2000–800BC
	Iron Age		800–AD43
	Roman		43–410
	Anglo Saxon		410–1066
	Norman		1066–1154
Medieval	Plantagenets		1154–1399
	Lancastrians		1399–1461
	Yorkists		1461–1485
Renaissance	Tudor		1485–1603
		Elizabethan	1558–1603
	Stuart		1603–1714
		Jacobean	1603–1649
		Commonwealth	1649–1660
		Restoration	1660–1702
		Queen Anne	1702–1714
	Hanoverian		1714–1901
		Georgian	1714–1837
		Regency	1810–1820
		Victorian	1837–1901
	Edwardian		1901–1910
	Windsor		1910–present

Index